PRAISE FOR *HOW TO KEEP GOOD TEACHERS AND PRINCIPALS*

"Dr. Melvin's book provides a thoughtful exploration of the changes educators are facing in classrooms and schools today. Her research suggests that students in our classrooms require more structured environments and approaches yet expect to have more autonomy and freedom to determine their own learning experiences. This is a synthesizing piece of work that will be helpful to anyone seeking to understand what is happening in education today."

—Sacra Nicholas, Ph.D., Instructional Leadership and
Academic Curriculum, University of Oklahoma

"Dr. Melvin has written a creative piece that illustrates many Oklahoma A+ concepts, including reflection, problem-solving, and action-oriented solutions, as she gives educators tips and suggestions that are practical and based on her expertise and professional experience. What a helpful approach!"

—Jean Hendrickson, Executive Director, Oklahoma A+ Schools,
University of Central Oklahoma

"*How to Keep Good Teachers and Principals* is a great source of information for educational professionals, parents, and mental health professionals alike. Dr. Melvin recognizes the importance of being strengths-based and consistent, and this philosophy is infused throughout the strategies that she outlines in this book; I think that nearly anyone working with children could benefit by reading it. I will definitely be buying a copy as soon as it is published, because what I've read so far is great!"

—Shannon Lee, B.A., mental health case manager

"American classrooms require significant changes if we are to prepare our children for the social, economic and political demands they will face in the twenty-first century. Dr. Lonnie Melvin provides a clear and concise, research-based dialogue that confronts the pressing issues that surround teaching and learning within this domain. *How to Keep Good Teachers and Principals* is a must-read for educators nationwide!"

—Goldie Thompson, minority teacher recruitment coordinator,
Oklahoma State Regents for Higher Education

"Not only are the solid, fundamental reasons for parent and family involvement clearly laid out . . . but also many concrete suggestions for accomplishing this involvement are shared. A great source for parents, school counselors, anyone new to the educational system . . . or for the experienced educator or principal looking for new ideas!"

—Libby Hatter, Washington Elementary PTA president,
Norman Public Schools, Norman, Oklahoma

"What a nice and worthwhile book! I never got bored with the topic, and as an educator, I was able to follow the rationale. Lots of current information and studies to lend validity. It is so obvious that Dr. Melvin is a highly educated source, presenting research and arguments that encourage educators to try news things with the Me Generation. I have enjoyed reading through your book. I am saying 'Amen' a lot! Definitely a valuable topic."

—Amy Dee Stephens, educator, author, and freelance writer

How to Keep Good Teachers and Principals

Practical Solutions to Today's Classroom Problems

Lonnie Melvin

ROWMAN & LITTLEFIELD EDUCATION

A division of

ROWMAN & LITTLEFIELD PUBLISHERS, INC.
Lanham • New York • Toronto • Plymouth, UK

Published by Rowman & Littlefield Education
A division of Rowman & Littlefield Publishers, Inc.
A wholly owned subsidiary of The Rowman & Littlefield Publishing Group, Inc.
4501 Forbes Boulevard, Suite 200, Lanham, Maryland 20706
http://www.rowmaneducation.com

Estover Road, Plymouth PL6 7PY, United Kingdom

Copyright © 2011 by Lonnie Melvin

Excerpts from *Where's the Learning in Service-Learning?* by Janet Eyler and Dwight E. Giles Jr. San Francisco: Jossey-Bass, 1999. Reprinted with permission of John Wiley & Sons, Inc.

"Non-retirement Leavers vs. Retirees" chart used by permission of the National Commission on Teaching America's Future.

Excerpts from www.rockman.com/articles/AuthenticLearning.htm used with permission of Saul Rockman.

All rights reserved. No part of this book may be reproduced in any form or by any electronic or mechanical means, including information storage and retrieval systems, without written permission from the publisher, except by a reviewer who may quote passages in a review.

British Library Cataloguing in Publication Information Available

Library of Congress Cataloging-in-Publication Data

Melvin, Lonnie, 1964–
How to keep good teachers and principals : practical solutions to today's classroom problems / Lonnie Melvin.
   p. cm.
Includes bibliographical references.
ISBN 978-1-60709-954-3 (cloth : alk. paper)—ISBN 978-1-60709-955-0 (pbk.: alk. paper)—ISBN 978-1-60709-956-7 (electronic)
1. Classroom management—United States. 2. School improvement programs—United States. 3. Educational leadership—United States. I. Title.
LB3013.M398 2011
371.2'07—dc22   2010039672

∞™ The paper used in this publication meets the minimum requirements of American National Standard for Information Sciences—Permanence of Paper for Printed Library Materials, ANSI/NISO Z39.48-1992.

Printed in the United States of America

Contents

Foreword		vii
Acknowledgments		ix
Introduction		1
Chapter 1	What Is Going On?	3
Chapter 2	So What Do Educators Do Now?	9
Chapter 3	Setting the Stage for Change	11
Chapter 4	Organizing Physical Space and Materials	13
Chapter 5	A Reflective Teaching Model	21
Chapter 6	Using My New Behavior Modification Model: Self-Correcting Behavior	25
Chapter 7	What Does Practice Look Like in a Self-Correcting Behavior Modification Model?	31
Chapter 8	Using Class Meetings to Build Success	35
Chapter 9	Creating a CSI (Critical Strategies Intervention) Classroom Using Technology	41
Chapter 10	Modeling as a Leader	49
Chapter 11	Practice during Recess	53
Chapter 12	Working with Parents	57
Chapter 13	Stabilizing and Maintaining a Consistent Environment	65

Chapter 14	Celebrating and Building Citizenship with Students	73
Chapter 15	Effective Teacher Evaluations: The New Performance-Based Model	79
Conclusion		87
Appendix A		89
Bibliography		91
About the Author		97

Foreword

Years ago, I heard the story of a school board in the Oklahoma Territory which determined that children learn best from pretty teachers. I have often wondered what the guidelines for such a policy would have been and who would have enforced them. As ludicrous as this policy might sound, in the past century, similar types of policies and procedures to evaluate teachers have abounded, and such evaluations have not always considered student learning. In fact, good principals, following district and state guidelines, have often noted the negative effects of mandates on teacher practices.

Since educational research has only recently been considered in establishing guidelines, personal experiences of policymakers have been the prime factor in making decisions. It isn't unheard of, for example, that because a fourth-grade teacher cannot answer a science question asked by the son of a legislator, new mandates are created. Indeed, subjective methodologies have led to many of the mandates that have been intended to improve teachers and principals over the years. Testing teachers for subject competency was one of the first requirements, which resulted in individuals as young as 16 being allowed to teach. Then came standards-based education, followed by educational requirements and bachelor's and master's degrees. Subsequently, certification and advanced certifications were added, and then more standards and testing. Each mandate was intended to guarantee that teachers could teach, and principals would evaluate to guarantee such.

Teachers and principals enter the profession to make a positive impact. Many see it as a calling—but teaching is complex. There are challenges that often cannot be anticipated. Principals have little preparation to evaluate good teaching and, more importantly, to analyze a problem a teacher may be having and to then give assistance so that the teacher can improve. Lacking these skills required for analyzing teaching practices has allowed ineffective teachers to remain in the classroom without any help in improving.

There is no question that having a high-quality education is imperative for all students, or for that to be a reality, effective principals and teachers are required. Educational opportunities are much different than they were even 25 years ago. Baby Boomers who remember a different educational reality—one that has radically changed—can throw impediments in the way of change. The younger generations, however, bring their own biases, actions, and attitudes which can likewise be impediments to the educational process.

As technologies evolve, the blackboard has given way to the Smartboard, and the filmstrip machine has become the DVD player. The four walls of the classroom have morphed into the Internet. The digital age makes it possible for students literally to go galactic—to learn more than ever possible in textbooks or in teacher lectures. Good teachers and principals have made it a point to appreciate and understand the impact of these new technologies and have adjusted their practices. Furthermore, effective teachers and principals are not necessarily born, but are molded through intentional, thoughtful analysis, critiquing, and modeling. Many, however, in frustration or confusion, have left the profession because they did not know how to make the adjustment.

Educational research, once almost non-existent and still certainly ignored, now plays an important role in implementing innovative practices. There have always been those teachers who designed creative programs that engaged students in relevant learning activities, but those practices were rarely shared or recognized to allow a broader scope of student learning to be realized. Utilizing research that validates practices is critical if educators are to move from recycling what has already been to imagining and implementing what has yet to be.

How does all of this translate into your world as a principal or teacher? In this book, Dr. Melvin has synthesized the issues and articulates research-based practices that have the power to have a positive impact on principals and teachers, and thus to improve student learning.

Kyle Dahlem
Oklahoma Educators Hall of Fame
DaVinci Board of Directors
Creative Oklahoma Board of Directors

Acknowledgments

I would like to thank all of my wonderful friends, who over the years supported me in all of my educational endeavors; my family, my colleagues, and the wonderful caring and loving staff at Madison Elementary. A big thank you to Linda, Karen, Pat, Michelle, Diana, and Connie who assisted me with edits. My friends, Amy and Jerry, who put a lot of love and support in the final edits and formatting; Kristin Wallace, who shared her gift and talent of art for the cover; and to Tom Koerner, the publisher with Rowman and Littlefield, who recognized the need for such a book. And last but not least, my dear friend, Karen, who convinced me to write the book.

Introduction

It is tough out there in education today. It seems that everyone I know who is a teacher, principal, or superintendent is stressed out and worn out. Between the current "Me" Generation, the overabundance of discipline problems and violence, the stress of the accountability measures of No Child Left Behind, and the current state of the economy, many of these professionals are retiring, changing jobs, or leaving the profession. This book serves as a wonderfully helpful hands-on toolbox to give educators more tools and strategies, including my own personally practiced version of a new behavior modification model called Self-Correcting Behavior Modification. Educators will find that this book will help them to get much-needed answers and relief to their continued attempt to try and serve as effectively and efficiently as possible with new techniques and activities, so that they do not have to leave their positions until they are ready.

How to Keep Good Teachers and Principals addresses student behavior, tools for teachers and principals, needs for professional development, identifies problems and how to incorporate new methods that work, and provides simple hands-on strategies that any school and staff can implement and do. It also includes my own creation of how-to's, strategies, and a useful behavior modification model I call the Self-Correcting Behavior Modification Model. The information presented here is based on my own experiences and research as an educator and educational leader. Having recently been in the classroom and schools, I am aware of the real current issues at hand, as well as what practical and applicable strategies teachers and principals can use that will work. This book includes new methods to use for implementation of much-needed behavior modification strategies, interventions, prevention, and instruction strategies and programs. Having a wide background in education, leadership, behavior management, and mental health, and having my own frustrations with the educational field today, I am able to give current educators a framework and practical solutions to set the stage for success in the classrooms today. In addition, this book will also be helpful to parents and mental health staff who work in schools and with children or their parents.

Chapter 1

What Is Going On?

This chapter outlines and describes the drastic changes we have had in education over the past few years, starting in the spring of 2006, and how these changes have affected teachers, principals, and superintendents, as well as many other educators from all over the United States, from rural America to urban cities, like never before.

Many educators are waking up every morning wondering what the heck has happened in education during the past few years. A new era seems to have arisen in this twenty-first century, in which things are definitely different, with many changes in both students and their needs.

All of a sudden, discipline issues have come to totally consume the time of both teachers and administrators, to the point of leaving little time for instruction. This has worn on educators, resulting in many leaving their positions for other jobs that are less stressful, or retiring from their school-based positions as teachers or principals; and even superintendents have been leaving in droves.

In 2005, television news reports announced to the nation that 1 out of every 10,000 students were being diagnosed with autism and Asperger Syndrome. Just three years later, that ratio would change to 1 out of every 150 students. The number of students being referred for special education and alternative schools has tripled. Schools have found themselves turning down transfers of new students from other districts due to the increasing number of special education referrals and the nationwide lack of special education teachers.

It has begun to seem that it is mostly boys who have been having major discipline problems at the elementary level; conversely, the middle school and high school levels have seen a rise in girls who have discipline problems.

What happened in society to cause this drastic change to occur? We have seen changes in education over the years, but this seems different, somehow.

Some administrators have thought these behavioral problems were a secondary factor caused by the war in Iraq and the separation and stress on the families. Some thought it was caused by the poor state of the economy and the stress associated with loss of jobs, fears of losing jobs, decreases in household income, and so forth. One interesting article from a medical journal even discussed how more mercury was being put into the immunization shots for children. Was that it? No matter what the reason, no matter what was going on, things were definitely different.

Teachers and administrators seemed to be at a stumbling block, trying to figure out what to do. Do I change my lesson plans? Do I integrate more technology? Do I attend more professional development? Do I retain these children? Do I refer them for special education testing? There seemed to be more questions than answers.

THE ME GENERATION

Today, current studies and many experts in educational news articles and books are talking about this new "Me" Generation, who is also referred to as Generation X. As described by the media, this is the new generation who are our current parents and their children.

These very intelligent young people have children at a young age. They are also very savvy with technology, able to text, e-mail, talk on the telephone, and take care of other business all at the same time. They seem to enjoy freedom and socialization, change jobs often, and may not attend college, a trend that is decreasing college enrollments across the nation for the first time in years.

The children of the "Me" Generation who are entering school seem to have a very independent spirits. They are very happy and carefree, but seem to have no boundaries to their behavior. They also do not seem to respond to the word "no," and want to set their own schedules. Many are exhibiting hitting and other aggressive behaviors that are causing great concern to schools and to parents whose children share such children's classes.

This state of affairs is causing many educators to regroup and look for alternative methods to use with students, and to look at the ways schools operate and classrooms are structured. Educators of twenty years have to drastically change the way they do things in the classroom; and new teachers are wondering, "What the heck did I get myself into?"

The numbers of incidents are growing. It is not just one or two students who have these issues. It is as high as three-quarters of the students in each class throughout a school—and the problem seems to be nationwide. The major problem seems to be with kindergarten students, who do not have the verbal skills to properly communicate and are using aggression instead.

After several years of dealing with this dilemma, teachers and administrators are worn out—they have exhausted all their ideas. And educators are continuing to retire and change jobs in record numbers.

A 2007 study by the NCTAF (National Commission on Teaching and America's Future) shows that schools across the nation are only retaining one-third of the new teachers for only up to one to two years, and that one-third of veteran teachers and other educators are retiring or changing to a nonschool job that is still in the education field, such as at state offices or educational consulting firms, or by teaching at the college level.

This means that only one-third of the teachers are consistently remaining in the schools. The NCTAF study shows that these teachers are in the middle of the bell curve on years of experience. They are too young to retire, and they have invested too many years to give up and leave now.

This is definitely a growing concern for administrators who are constantly looking for new staff replacements, and who are also concerned about the morale of the teachers and schools. The current economy contributes to the problem with the lack of educational dollars and the increasing risk of having larger class sizes and fewer staff members.

So what do we do now? Superintendents are finding that even the most effective districts are losing good teachers and principals. For the first time, it seems that giving pay raises does not seem to make a difference in trying to keep good educators. The conventional wisdom, which says that offering these teachers higher salaries will encourage them to stay, is wrong.

Pay is not the deciding factor when it comes to why so many new teachers are leaving the classrooms. NCTAF (2007) believes that we need to go a step further to look at a support systems for new teachers, the Cross-Generational Mentoring program. This program is designed to keep highly qualified and effective veteran teachers on staff to work with and mentor new teachers.

Superintendents, principals, and teachers may also be willing to voluntarily take pay cuts to keep staff and programs. However, they know they cannot do this alone anymore, and with the large number of students with discipline issues, many are afraid to be alone in the rooms with the students without some help.

According to the NCTAF research of April 2007, a national survey of teachers and principals showed that the nation stands to lose half of its teachers to retirement in the next decade. Furthermore, the report found that over 50% of teachers and principals were Baby Boomers.

Baby Boomers are the generation who grew up with a strong work ethic and were hard workers. It was a generation of "helpers and nurturers," with many of the youth going into helping professions, especially teaching. Baby Boomers were planners and organized their lives for the future. Many of them became educational leaders; more women went into administration than in any previous era.

What does this new "Me" Generation do to the Baby Boomers? It throws them for a loop! The Baby Boomers find themselves struggling with the "Me" Generation, not exactly knowing what to do with them.

All of the tricks of the trade that Baby Boomers try as teachers are not necessarily working with the "Me" Generation. This is not a group who likes to follow rules or do the right thing just because they are told to do so. This will be a generation who will break boundaries to establish their own guidelines and thoughts.

How in the world will we work with this generation? We will have to pull new tricks out of our hats and attend more professional development to learn what to try. The cost of teacher and principal turnover could be outrageous! The consistency and retainability of staff will surely drop. At times, it seems as if there are more new staff in some buildings than there are veteran staff.

Will this undermine our ability to close the achievement gap? Will this create a teacher and principal retention crisis? Will it affect the quality of teaching or leadership in the schools?

Just because staff are called highly qualified, are they really? Are we keeping a good amount of effective veteran teachers in the schools to serve as mentors to the younger teachers? Or are we losing this important piece of the educational framework that has been so successful for schools historically?

Some districts and states have implemented teacher mentoring programs over the years for their schools and teachers. Are these mentoring programs alone enough to maintain the high quality of educators in the profession, or do we need to look at new options or opportunities? NCTAF's research shows that we will lose one-third of our accomplished educators over the next four years, equating to over 100,000 educators making a mass exodus. Figure 1 shows the trends in teacher attrition from 1987 to 2004.

This chapter discusses the drastic changes educators have seen over the past few years, and how these changes have affected all educators, including teachers, principals, and superintendents. The needs and discipline issues of students of the twenty-first century are consuming the time of teachers and administrators until they leave little time for instruction. This has eventually worn on the educators, resulting in many leaving their positions for other jobs

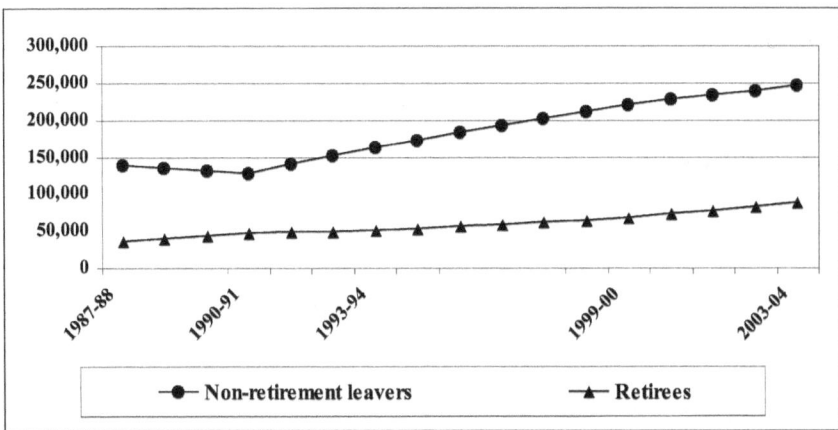

Figure 1.1.

that are less stressful, or retiring from their school-based positions as teachers or principals; even superintendents have been leaving in droves.

Those educators who want to stay employed in the schools are drastically changing the way they do things in the classroom, trying to regroup and look for alternative methods to use with the students, and to look at the way that schools operate and that classrooms are structured. A program such as NCTAF's Cross-Generational Mentoring assists in keeping the highly qualified and effective veteran teachers on staff to work with and mentor the new teachers.

Chapter 2

So What Do Educators Do Now?

Even the most qualified educators are finding the changes in this era difficult and challenging. This chapter discusses how merely recruiting new staff will not get us out of this dilemma. It will take much more. High-poverty schools seem to be the hardest hit of the school populations, but non-title schools are not immune to this crisis.

Being a principal and talking with colleagues across the nation, it seems the traditional teaching career is collapsing at both ends. Both beginning and veteran teachers, as well as educational leaders, are being driven away by antiqued preparation practices, outdated school policies and procedures, a lack of resources for teachers and students, and an increase in discipline issues. It is time for a change.

In an effort to assist in sustaining and educating highly qualified educators, universities have become proactive in the quest to produce quality teacher and leader candidates who are ready to walk into the classroom or a school and teach or lead. They are working closely in collaborative efforts with school districts to produce academically high-quality new teachers and leaders.

Educators have more opportunities to do student internships earlier and more often than in the past, when student teaching and internships only occurred in the last semester before graduating from college. Opportunities now exist each semester in block classes, field studies, and internships throughout the college career.

The only criteria that seems to still be lacking with the new teacher candidates is the experience with classroom management. The universities typically focus on content and methods in education but—to their credit—are implementing newer courses with content such as parent and community involvement, recognizing this as a need. When asked, most teacher candidates will tell you that they typically have one course in classroom management during college. This is just not enough to prepare new teachers for what is going on in the classrooms today.

In the past few decades, school districts, universities, state departments of education, and educational unions have discovered and implemented new teacher mentoring and induction programs. Research has shown that mentoring programs can effectively assist new teachers to get acclimated into the educational environment, become familiar and competent with the curriculum and expectations of the school, master the state standards, and increase the overall competence of the teacher. This, in turn, directly impacts student achievement.

If new teachers are assigned an effective veteran mentor who is proficient in classroom management, the new teacher will have a much higher rate of success with his or her own classroom management. If the new teacher does not have an effective veteran mentor who is proficient in classroom management, the new teacher will struggle with classroom management and, research says, will usually leave teaching within two years.

This is an immediate concern of NCTAF and many educational leaders across the country. Losing good veteran teachers and educators, as well as our new teacher candidates, will only compound the problems we are dealing with in education today. Being able to keep our high-quality veteran educators will provide the seamless mentoring and induction process that can be highly effective in the transition from being a new teacher to becoming an effective and highly qualified veteran teacher.

Educational leaders do worry about the veteran teachers and educators who are worn out, stressed out, and want to retire but have put their plans on hold due to the economy and low income they would receive from teacher retirement. They are aware that these educators are not giving 100 percent to the position anymore and are not practicing as highly qualified educators. These educators are not considered good mentor candidates for new educators. They are not effective due to their current situation and do not provide good mentoring skills and assistance to new teachers.

Chapter 2 discusses how important it is to keep high-quality teachers and principals in a school and district. When schools and districts lose their most qualified teachers and administrators, this not only depletes veteran educational staff, but also depletes the districts of precious dollars that could be put into the improvement of quality education and student achievement. As all committed educators are aware, a strong collaborative educational environment and staff are at the heart of every successful school and district.

Chapter 3

Setting the Stage for Change

"There are two ways to deal with change: wait and the change will come to you or create the change you want. It is time to create the change we want to see" (NCTAF 2009). U.S. Secretary of Education Arne Duncan (2009) calls on the nation's educational leaders to think very creatively and to think very differently. This chapter will discuss how this is the time to empower school leaders and teachers as agents of change, rather than as targets of change.

Looking at the needs of our educational populations today, it appears that pre-kindergarten through 12th-grade student enrollment is on the rise nationwide. As a result, districts are building new schools and the economy is dictating larger class sizes. State-standardized test scores and average yearly progress (AYP) continue to be a high priority, but many are concerned about how the No Child Left Behind (NCLB) mandates affect the populations of special education students, ELL (English Language Learner) students, and Title I schools.

As Duncan and President Obama revisit NCLB, professional educators across the country are hoping that things will change in education and get better. Newspaper articles quoting Duncan and President Obama describe the possibility of implementing a growth model in education.

THINKING ABOUT A NEW ASSESSMENT

A growth model typically allows educators to track the growth of each child independently versus comparing last year's tests scores for a particular group or grade level against this year's test scores of a different group. For educators, that model is comparing apples and oranges and puts the focus and accountability on the teacher and not on the academic growth of the child.

The Center for Public Education in Virginia (2007) states that growth models can help schools and districts see just how much academic progress their students are making by measuring progress between two points in time.

Although schools are held accountable for student achievement, many educators and researchers believe that reporting student growth provides a more accurate picture of school effectiveness than the current snapshot of achievement, due to its not taking into account where a student started academically. It is also the only model designed to determine which aspect of schooling (e.g., school, teacher, and education program) is responsible for a student's growth.

A very mobile student population exists in education today. Each month sees students move to a new school or state, making it almost impossible for educators to make much progress with the students. Many educators, such as myself, would like to see the educational focus of NCLB change to become *Teach Every Child*, with a focus on the children—the important ones who really matter. They are our future.

Teachers do not have a problem being accountable for teaching a child, but they want to be able to measure growth for the amount of time they have each child in their care. A growth model allows teachers to do that. Teachers will be responsible and held accountable for what they teach each child, and what each child learns during the time they have them. Growth is measured by giving a pretest upon entry, weekly or monthly assessments, and a posttest upon completion of the time with that teacher.

As with any model, teachers in a building should continue to work together collaboratively with their students using needed support programs such as Title I math or reading labs, ELL instruction, special education labs, and so forth in the continuation of academic excellence.

Focused professional development will need to be a strong component of the new growth model for education. The Center for Public Education (2007) discusses how important it is to provide "targeted training to all stakeholders including teachers, principals, school board members, administrators, parents, and students, to help them understand exactly what is being measured and how to use the information effectively."

The belief in chapter 3 is that growth models can be sophisticated tools that help gauge how much student learning is currently taking place. Investing in high-quality education, as well as current and accurate assessment procedures for each individual student, can yield benefits for students, schools, and communities, as well as retaining our good teachers, principals, and superintendents. This is a model educators could stand behind, support, and be accountable for, because not only is it realistic—it makes sense.

Chapter 4

Organizing Physical Space and Materials

Harry Wong (2001) believes that what you do on the first days of school will determine your success or failure for the rest of the school year. Chapter 4 discusses how to structure a successful first day of school and set the stage for an effective classroom and a successful school year.

ORGANIZING YOUR SPACE

Effective teachers spend time organizing and structuring their classrooms so that the students know what to do to succeed and carry out the same consistency daily throughout the year. This is very important to do because of the high number of discipline issues schools are having, the increasing number of special education children in the classrooms, and the rise of children with autism being mainstreamed in the classrooms.

Establish Consistency

The most important thing to do in a classroom is to establish consistency. This procedure works well for the "Me" Generation. These students need routines with specific guidelines including steps, and directions. Directions should be visible, posted on the board, displayed using PowerPoint, or written on a piece of paper and handed to them. Some teachers tape a student's daily schedule on the student's desk for quick viewing. This method helps those students who stress over "what comes next."

The students these days want to know what is happening and what they are getting. Many students do not want surprises or disorganization, and do not handle it well. This leads to classroom management problems. As a principal, I could recognize good classroom management and consistency upon observation when I walked into a classroom. I would observe students to see if they knew the routines, knew what to expect, and looked at the board to see if the objectives were written on it.

This Will Lead to Problems!

Consistent routines must be established prior to the first day of school and remain consistent throughout the year. Inconsistency and disorganization causes discipline problems. Nothing will drive a teacher to contemplate a career change faster than an out-of-control classroom.

If a teacher tries to organize the room and activities as the year goes on, he or she will lose control of the classroom and students. That procedure no longer works with the "Me" Generation. A teacher has to be on his or her toes, prepared, organized, and ready to teach the lesson each day. Many administrators have seen an increase in discipline issues when a teacher does not have good classroom management and organized structure to routines and lessons for the day.

Harry Wong (2001) states, "You increase the chance of student success and decrease the chance of student disruptions if the materials, classroom climate, and teacher are ready before the students arrive. A routine is what the student does automatically without prompting or supervision. Thus, a routine becomes a habit, practice, or custom for the student."

Teachers today are already stressed with the number of students in their classrooms, the number of discipline issues, and the high number of special needs students. Being unorganized in a classroom today just adds to the chaos and stress, and makes for an unsafe classroom.

Many of the students in the "Me" Generation are coming into the classrooms and schools without boundaries and are physically violent, hitting, kicking, biting, punching, and so forth. Schools are seeing not only an increase of discipline issues, but also a new era of teachers and parents pressing charges on other students for violent behaviors. This is happening as early as pre-kindergarten and kindergarten age classes, due to the large amounts of violent behaviors with the younger students.

Kevin Harris (1995) quotes Albert Einstein: "We cannot solve problems by using the same kind of thinking we used when we created them." Establishing routines and having class organization and consistency will save time as well as emotional wear and tear on both the teachers and students.

Take an Inventory of the Classroom

Teachers will want to take an inventory of their classrooms to make sure that the materials being used in the classrooms are safe and could not injure another student. Items such as scissors should probably have blunt ends and any items that could be unsafe should be locked away and only used with appropriate and specific directions and supervision. The "Me" Generation students seems to do better with a clean space that is organized. These students like their own space, as well as sometimes a quiet space to go to when needed.

Organizational skills may also be difficult for students with learning disabilities or autism, or any student who has not learned "how to be organized." Gathering the required materials for a class project or packing up the necessary items to go home might be complex tasks for students, as they require a simultaneous focus on both the immediate situation, as well as a focus on future and desired outcomes (Mesibov, Shea & Schopler 2005). Teachers can provide a checksheet for the student with a list of the materials to gather in order and what to do with them once you get them. Assigning a "help buddy" to the student at the beginning of the year provides additional initial assistance until the student feels more confident and less stressed when getting the materials themselves.

A disorganized classroom space may complicate the successful completion of tasks for students with learning disabilities or autism, and may inhibit a student's ability to perform independently. These students do not like or do well with a lot of noise, crowds or crowded spaces, or a lack of organization. Providing visual schedules and consistent routines for these students helps to maximize their learning and minimize their stress levels.

Accessorize for "Me!"

Teachers and principals should consider having items in the classrooms such as napping mats, bean bag chairs, and rocking chairs for those students who might need to take a break or who cannot sit still. The mat and bean bag chair allows for a rest time, and the rocking chairs allow movement without moving around in a crowded classroom and disturbing other students.

Establish organizational systems in the classroom at the beginning of the year and teach all students how to use them. Designating clear locations for specific materials such as homework, notes home, school supplies, and personal items is helpful, as well as creating routines around "when and how to turn in" items. A structured classroom benefits all students, including students with special education disorders and learning disabilities.

How the Classroom Is Arranged Can Make a Big Difference!

With the recent increase in the number of children with autism, it is important to establish a supportive classroom environment for students when planning and implementing instruction. Research has consistently indicated that the way the classroom environment is arranged influences the learning of individuals, including students with learning disabilities and autism (Hurth, Shaw, Izeman, Whaley, & Rogers 1999). Students with autism may have difficulty gaining meaning from their activities, experiences, and/or environment (Mesibov, Shea, & Schopler 2005).

Additionally, research has found that students in organized and structured classrooms demonstrate more on-task behavior and higher academic achievement (Heflin & Alberto 2001). Whether students are served in general education settings, self-contained settings, or any combination of locations, an organized classroom is the first place to start.

A student's participation may currently be limited due to a student not understanding what is expected of him or her in a specific area of the classroom, or during an instructional activity. An organized classroom with defined areas and spaces can assist a student in anticipating the requirements of a specific setting and to predict what will be happening during the instructional day. This reduces the stress of the student drastically and allows the student the freedom to make better choices, as well as possibly limiting any violent behavior.

Distractions, Distractions, Distractions!

Distractibility may also be a challenge for students, especially children with autism or learning disabilities. Students may be focusing on a variety of sensations they are experiencing (i.e., sounds, sights, smells), and have difficulty prioritizing the importance of the information presented in the environment. A disorganized classroom can pull a student's attention to irrelevant details and interrupt his or her ability to sustain focus. Providing an environment that minimizes competing distractions and is free of extraneous stimuli and clutter can assist students in attending to relevant information.

Organizing a classroom also means minimizing the auditory and visual distractions. This helps students to focus on the concepts that are being taught instead of on details that may not be relevant, and reduces competing distractions. Often when students, especially students with learning disabilities or autism, are presented with too much stimulus (visual or auditory), processing may slow down or, if overloaded, may stop completely. This is a natural response.

Consider the bulletin board used for announcements in the teacher's lounge, church lobby, or at the grocery store. When information is presented in an orderly fashion and the space is not cluttered, we are much more likely to read and digest the information than when the board is overloaded. When papers are stacked on top of one another and the space is disorderly, we are likely to pass by the bulletin board without processing any of the information.

Minimizing distractions involves considering how much information is posted on classroom walls and determining whether what is posted is relevant to the class activity. Teachers may consider reducing the amount of stimuli in the classroom, or may decide to hang the information out of the field of vision of the most distractible students (i.e., behind the students, in a center area that doesn't require as much attention or focus).

Putting all extraneous materials and supplies in cabinets, boxes, drawers, or folders is beneficial, and covering open shelves with solid colored fabric can be helpful as well. Considering sources of noise like the hallway, playground, cafeteria, bathroom, and intercom is also important when organizing classroom spaces.

Similarly, visual distractions like windows, doorways, reflective surfaces, fans, computer screens, ceiling decorations, and classroom traffic should be assessed when designing the classroom space to meet the needs of all of the students. Often, these distractions can be easily covered with butcher paper, fabric, cardboard, or the item or student can be moved to a better location.

Establish Boundaries

There are several key concepts to consider when organizing your classroom for all students. The first is to create clear physical and/or visual boundaries to help students know where "each area begins and ends." Segmenting the environment helps clarify the expectations. Once students are taught expected behaviors for each space in the classroom, the distinct areas become powerful cues for appropriate behavior.

Boundaries may also help communicate to younger students, or those who are impulsive or motor-driven, where each area begins and ends and where they are supposed "to be or stay in" during specific activities. These boundaries are not intended to "contain" students, as most of them can be easily climbed over or walked around; they are simply intended to establish cues about classroom spaces and expectations.

Secondly, the teacher will want to identify the different areas he or she would like to create in the classroom. These typically relate to what curriculum areas are addressed, the age level of the students, and what activities will occur in the classroom space.

Many teachers, both in general education and special education classrooms, design areas for teacher-directed activities (often individual desks), small and large group activities (i.e., small tables, carpet space on the floor), centers (i.e., reading corner, computers), and, often, small spaces for individual instruction or independent work if needed. Other classroom spaces may include areas to address leisure skills, vocational skills, self-help and self-management skills, and sensory development.

Next, the teacher will want to segment the different areas using the boundaries or visual cues. The types of boundaries used may vary depending on the age of the students, the students' familiarity with structured classrooms, the classroom setting, and the strengths and needs of individual students.

Use What You Have

Boundaries can be created with the furniture found in the classroom, such as desks, shelves, filing cabinets, or tables, as well as with teacher-created materials such as fabric, cardboard table-top dividers, or masking tape. Visual cues, like colored rugs, labels, color coding, highlighting, or placemats, are helpful in differentiating areas as well, especially locations that may be used for more than one purpose.

Practice Makes Perfect

The final step is to teach students how to move through the classroom space, as well as what the expectations are for each segmented area. This may involve pointing out the boundaries and visual cues to students, practicing how to respond to the cues, and completing activities in each classroom space with guidance. This step also requires teachers to evaluate the spaces they have designed and determine whether the boundaries are meaningful for the students.

If students have continued difficulty following classroom expectations, the teacher may decide that the organization of the classroom needs to be modified. For example, if the teacher has placed tape on the floor to delineate a boundary in the reading center, and the student peels off the tape or frequently leaves the center without being cued, the staff may decide that the visual cue used is not meaningful, and that a bookshelf may be more appropriate.

Chapter 4 discusses how the organizational needs of students vary by individual. A continual assessment of how the classroom environment is impacting the student's behavior and attention is required by the teacher. Regular organizational changes may need to be made throughout the school year as the teacher gets to know the students and students are enrolled and dropped.

The main questions an educator should ask at the beginning of the year and all year long are, Is the classroom ready for learning? and Does the organization of the classroom and routines meet the needs of all of the students? This kind of organization allows the teacher to feel adequate and in control of the classroom, as well as to create the atmosphere to provide more quality instruction. It also takes the stress off of the teacher and puts the fun and focus back into learning.

Chapter 5

A Reflective Teaching Model

This chapter discusses how important it is for an educational system to maintain a reflective inquiry-based instructional approach, not only with behaviors, routines, and class structures, but also as a focus in the teaching approach to continue to build a foundation on the human functions of learning and behavior and construct meaning from information, experience, reflections, and model and practice.

A model, such as the Reflective Teaching Model developed by Eastern Mennonite University (1996), can be used to address professional knowledge bases in the classroom such as knowledge of self, knowledge of content, knowledge of teaching and learning, knowledge of pupils, and knowledge of context within schools and society. This model continues the same focus on student-centered learning, but with instruction, inquiry, and reflection as the focus. In classrooms today, teachers must be prepared to work with all students considering all needs, classroom management and structure, and diverse populations in an ever-changing twenty-first-century cultural and global context that requires teachers who are adequately trained, highly qualified, knowledgeable, caring, and responsive.

WHAT IS THE REFLECTIVE TEACHING MODEL?

Reflective Teaching is a method that uses an inquiry approach that emphasizes an ethic of caring, a constructivist approach to teaching, and creative problem solving. An ethic of caring respects the wonderful range of multiple talents and capacities of all individuals, regardless of cultural, intellectual, or gender differences. A premium is placed on the dignity of all persons.

Teachers, using a constructivist approach, place emphasis on big concepts, student questions, active learning, and cooperative learning. Teachers interweave assessment with teaching while using reflection practices to determine learning.

A constructivist approach is an approach that seeks to connect theory to practice and views the student as a "thinker, creator, and constructor." Integral to a constructivist theory of learning is creative problem solving. Teachers take responsibility for assessing and solving problems; not with mechanistic "cookbook" recipes, but by asking: What decisions should I be making? On what basis do I make these decisions? and What can I do to enhance learning? (Eastern Mennonite University 2009).

How Does the Reflective Teaching Model Integrate Theory with Practice?

In the Reflective Teaching Model, learning is based on the teacher asking significant questions in the context of experiences. It incorporates reflective thinking and teaching into a sequential curriculum pattern with initiatory, developmental, and culminating phases by asking the following five questions:

- Exploring Teaching: *Shall I Teach?*
- Academic Preparation: *What Shall I Teach?*
- Understanding Learners: *How Do Students Learn?*
- Organizing for Teaching: *How Shall I Teach?*
- Schooling and Cultural Context: *Why Do We Teach?*

Teachers should utilize instructional activities such as cooperative learning strategies, class interaction, centers, technology, and differentiated instruction. Special attention should be given to the application of theory and practice by helping students make connections between relevant concepts through higher-order questioning strategies and reflective thinking skills, having the ability to evaluate and interpret evidence, modify views, and make objective judgments.

Sparks-Langer (1992) discusses how the Reflective Teaching Model should not be viewed as a simplistic "fix-it" model whereby a solution is developed to correct a problem without addressing the underlying causes of the problem. Rather, it examines underlying assumptions and becomes a useful model to understand the interaction of dispositions (being), practice (doing), and professional knowledge (knowing). At the heart of the model is a cyclical process leading to the construction of meaning. Meaning is constructed when awareness is created by observing and gathering information by (1) analyzing the information to identify any implications, (2) hypothesizing to explain the events and guide further action, (3) implementing an action plan, and (4) evaluating the results.

In order to be effective, a unified effort must be made in the school by all staff to implement these strategies. Focused professional development is an important piece of this structure to educate all staff, including the support staff, of the vision, mission, purpose, and strategies of reflective learning, for which model and practice of the behaviors are instrumental.

Sandra Gupton summarizes this chapter well by discussing how educational leaders cannot do it alone, especially nowadays. Just as it takes a village to raise a child, it takes an entire faculty to educate a student body and ensure academic excellence. Gupton (2003) discusses how effective leaders do not facilitate change and improve schools alone. All school personnel must treat change as a complex and constant learning process, not as an event. The only thing constant is change itself, especially in education.

Chapter 6

Using My New Behavior Modification Model: Self-Correcting Behavior

Thomas Sergiovanni (1991), researcher and author, contends that a "good principal needs to have some sense of what she or he values, have something to be committed to, a compass to help navigate the way—a personal vision" (p. 334). This chapter discusses how educational leaders in a district or school need to have a clear focus of what needs to be done in their buildings and for their schools, considering the abrupt changes going on with the overwhelming discipline issues and the changes in society.

Not only will I discuss different kinds of behavior management models, but I will also introduce my own practiced and researched behavior modification model, the Self-Correcting Behavior Modification Model, in this chapter as a tool to use for this dilemma. Based on my experience and research, I have combined a number of successful theories that work well with the "Me" Generation. The following chapters also address my Self-Correcting Behavior Modification Model:

- Chapter 7: What Does Practice Look Like in a Self-Correcting Behavior Modification?
- Chapter 8: Using Class Meetings to Build Success
- Chapter 11: Practice during Recess

In today's world, to be successful in schools, educational leaders need to implement a strategy of utilizing a model and practice approach, as well as establish a long-range plan to use this model in their schools to combat the overwhelming discipline issues that are currently in the schools. Along with this, specific and focused professional development for the staff is necessary to also address the issues at hand. Topics for professional development might range from behavior modification strategies, classroom management, utilizing class meetings in the classrooms, building collaborative relationships with parents, designing lesson plans to incorporate twenty-first-century learning for students, and so forth.

Many branches and schools of thought, with varying terminology in regards to behavior management, exist today. Schwahn and Spady (1998) stated, "Effective leaders reflect deeply on their values and principles, are open to their organization and the public about them, and consistently model them" (p. 73). Establishing a new behavioral management system, providing focused professional development, and modeling and monitoring the new model being used are important to the success of the model.

Sergiovanni and Starratt (1983) propose that leaders develop an educational platform that would describe the atmosphere and climate as one that encompasses "the assumptions or beliefs that deal with the way children and youth grow, with the purposes of schooling, with the nature of learning, with pedagogy and teaching, with educational programs, and with school climate" (p. 27).

Schools all over the country have begun to address student and behavior management issues, using many different methods and strategies. Many schools have brought in professional speakers or have begun other behavior management and intervention programs such as Response to Intervention Training (RTI) or Positive Behavior Intervention Support (PBIS/PBS).

Other schools address returning and newly hired teachers with their own form of professional development ideas and opportunities utilizing professional staff from the school such as the principal, school counselor, school psychologist, and other school or district personnel to present their ideas for behavior management strategies for the upcoming year.

Behavior modification, or "behavior management," as it is known today in schools, was developed by Pavlov in the early part of the twentieth century. This therapy model was adapted by John Watson in 1920 and was eventually translated into behavior therapy by researchers and clinicians such as B. F. Skinner and Hans Eysenck in the 1950s, and into cognitive behavior therapy by researchers such as Donald Meichenbaum.

Behavior modification models have been used in education for a long time, and have been used for quite some time in both inpatient and outpatient mental health treatment facilities. Some teachers around the country have used a behavior management model for years as a classroom management technique along with the accountability behavior model. Programs as early as in the elementary levels, for example, use behavior modification for approaches with student discipline to teach students to learn how to make appropriate decisions.

Some educators have used more components of the behavior modification model than others, not always fully implementing the model. Special education teachers have probably used the behavior management model more often than the regular education teachers due to the nature of what they do in emotionally disturbed (ED or SED) labs and classrooms as well as in other types of special education programs such as learning disabled (LD) labs and speech pathology.

The accountability behavior model has been in place since even before the 1990s, but just doesn't seem to be working with the "Me" Generation. These students do not seem to really care about being made accountable. The accountability behavior model is actually making the situation worse, with students acting out more than normal, rebelling against the very concept of accountability. This model addresses the behavior of students by stating not only the behavior violation, as well as the expected behavior that should have occurred, but also the consequence for inappropriate behavior. For example, when a student is kicking another student at recess, the teacher calls the student over and discusses the situation and what appropriate behavior should happen, such as asking a teacher for help instead of kicking a student in anger. The student who kicked then sits out during recess for a certain amount of time, depending on what is developmentally appropriate.

In the accountability model, students are given consequences based on the severity of the offense, as well as the behavioral step the student may be on. Our current students are no longer responding to the accountability model. The students seem to need a model that would "teach or train" them on what skills they need to know to have appropriate behavior. This accountability model seems to still be effective at times with children who understand and accept consequences, which, in the past, were the majority of the students in a school. The students who "bucked" the system and acted out typically were the minority in the past.

Over the years, schools across the country have had success with similar models that are a combination of accountability and behavior management, such as Jim Faye's Love and Logic Model (2009). Faye's model is based on the theory of addressing students' behavior in a way that lets students know that you love and care about them while stating the desired expectations and appropriate behavior and then giving consequences or warnings to the child. A parental component to Jim Faye's Love and Logic model is available for parents to use at home with their children to teach their children how to adopt appropriate behavior.

Educators all around the country have begun to discuss what to do about our current generation and the discipline and violence issues that have evolved in the schools. It seems that we need to move away from the old accountability model, which is not working with our new generation, to a new type of model. I am suggesting a new model that I developed and with which I have experimented, called the Self-Correcting Behavior Modification Model.

The Self-Correcting Behavior Management model is a non-shame-based model that focuses on the inappropriate behavior, not on the person. This model emphasizes the separation of personhood and behavior.

A student does not equal his or her behavior; behavior is just a student's actions, and can be changed by better decision-making. Personhood is "who" a person is fundamentally: his or her moral base. This is usually who the person is born as, his or her values and morals, and the foundation of what he or she believes. Personhood can be both learned and inherited.

Some resiliency studies show us that some people are just born the way they are. They may have the will to survive under any circumstances or to do the right thing, because they have a strong belief about doing so. Separating personhood from behavior is important to the self-esteem of the student. Through this strategy, students learn that who they are is "who they are inside": their beliefs, their motivations, and what drives them.

It is important to teach the students that behavior is an immediate and specific decision made at the time: a different, better decision can be made next time. Making a bad decision does not make a student a bad person; it just means that a bad decision is correctable. With resources and education, a better decision can be made in the future. Establishing a system of modeling and practicing the intended behavior is important for the implementation of Self-Correction Behavior Modification, which is discussed more in detail, with examples, in chapters 7, 8, and 11.

A CHANGE IN A PRINCIPAL'S ROLE

The last fifteen years or so have seen a shift to a view of the principal as more of a democratic leader who engages staff in the empowerment and collaboration process in decisions regarding the school and students. Gupton (2003) believes that this type of leadership and facilitation creates a learning and collaborative community rather than a "unilateral, autocratic environment complete with top-down authoritarian commands of the principal" (p. 23).

Principals can no longer handle discipline by themselves; the job is just too big. Leaders need the help of the teachers to implement research-based behavior modification strategies that work with the students of the twenty-first century. Implementing strategies such as the Self-Correction Behavior Modification Model in the classrooms, in the cafeteria, on the playground, and so forth works to change behavior and is conducive to "teaching" appropriate behavior versus punishing inappropriate behavior.

When first using the Self-Correcting Behavior Management Model, it is productive for educators to first consider the stressors of each student in their current class and life. Stress has been discussed many times when addressing adults, but is very rarely discussed in terms of children and how it impacts them, their behavior, and their learning.

In 1986, Antoinette Saunders and Bonnie Remsberg published a book called *The Stress-Proof Child*. This book emphasizes the impact that various changes have on the life of a child. Children react to stress in different ways, many times acting out as a result of too much stress. Appendix A includes a stress test and scale that could assist the teachers in identifying stressors that their students might have. Factors include being a new student, having moved to a new town, a parent's having lost a job, a parent's being in the military and out of the country, the arrival of a new baby sister or brother, struggles with reading or math, feeling as if one will never fit in with his or her peers, and so on.

When piloting the use of appendix A recently at an elementary school where I was the principal, the teachers discovered that their students have the same or similar stressors as adults do. The students simply do not have the maturity or the skills to know what to do, how to handle the situations. Many times this results in acting out, hitting, kicking, biting, fighting, violence, shutdowns, or hurting others.

The younger the students are, the fewer verbal skills and resources they have. Schools have noticed many of the young students, such as pre-kindergarteners and kindergarteners, hitting students, kicking, biting, and throwing things more often than previous years. And many times these days, it is as much as half to three-quarters of the class exhibiting this behavior, which causes a lot of stress for the educational staff.

Author Sandra Gupton (2003) explains that implementing a new educational platform, plan, model, or system is not easy. Even veteran educators sometimes find it difficult to commit to what they believe about these important changes, and whether they think they will work in a school.

The chapter discusses how important it is to adopt and implement your own behavior management system in your school, such as the Self-Correction Behavior Modification Model. Doing so will require a great deal of reflection and introspection, and may require some reading and research as you stumble about for responses that make sense to you when you actually see them on paper. But it is a tool you must have to be your best as an educator; without one, you will have great difficulty succeeding as a school leader and principal.

Chapter 7

What Does Practice Look Like in a Self-Correcting Behavior Modification Model?

"Today's educators must embrace both organizational and human concerns in order to maximize the school's effectiveness" (Gupton 2003, p. 22). This chapter discusses the technique of model and practice with student behavior when using the Self-Correction Behavior Modification Model. Consistent use of this model teaches, and allows, students to have the opportunity to learn more about appropriate behavior and how to make better decisions. These researched and practiced techniques help minimize the reoccurring discipline issues in a school and take the stress off of the school staff.

Today, many "Me" Generation students seem to be able to make their own decisions often. They are given many choices—something that can be good or bad. Too many choices set the stage for allowing a student to be in control of the situation. Limiting choices can provide a focus for the expected behavior of the child. Thus, the choices given to a child should be carefully thought out. It is not wise to give children choices that you know are not productive and that will not give you the intended outcome that you desire as an adult, parent, teacher, or principal.

When piloting the Self-Correction Behavior Modification Model at a school, the staff stated that the techniques and strategies were successful for giving children choices and addressing behavioral issues. The goal of the Self-Correction Behavior Modification Model is to change and adjust behavior that is inappropriate or undesirable in some way to a more desirable and appropriate behavior. When implementing the Self-Correction Behavior Modification Model with a teen or child, it is important that the undesirable behavior be isolated and observed, with limited choices provided. It is vital to provide modeling and practicing of the appropriate behaviors expected, as well as constant positive communication with the students.

With observation and use of this strategy, comes awareness of the behavior on the part of the parent or teacher, as well as on the part of the individual student whose behavior is being modified. With this new awareness also comes the greater goal of understanding the cause and effect of the behaviors, thus helping to effect change. Self-Correction Behavior Modification also works well with students who have been diagnosed with ADD, ADHD, and conduct disorders, as well as other types of emotional and learning disorders or disabilities.

A successful program of child behavior modification, such as Self-Correcting Behavior Modification Model, must have consistency in order to be effective (National Youth Network 2009). Ann Lieberman (1995) discusses how "leadership calls for principals to act as partners with teachers, involved in a collaborative quest to examine practices, and improve schools . . . Principals are not expected to control teachers and students, but to support them and to create opportunities for them to grow and develop" (p. 55).

As educators, we know how important modeling is for students, but do we do it enough, or do we just tell students what to do? Research says that modeling ingrains the behavior four to five times more efficiently than merely verbally instructing a student. Roland Barth (1990), researcher and author, suggests that, "our behavior becomes reflexive, inconsistent, and shortsighted as we seek the action that will most quickly put out the fire so we can get on with putting out the next one" (p. 211).

In education today, teachers are so overwhelmed with responsibilities and duties. Teachers feel as if they are in triage mode daily, just trying to survive the day or the moment. That is not good for anyone.

During the first week of school each year, educators around the country practice and inform students of rules and procedures. It now appears that taking only the first week to go over and practice the rules with the students is just not enough. The "Me" Generation needs a month or longer at the beginning of the year, along with constant modeling and practicing during the year, especially if new activities are introduced.

The students need more "practice" to solidify the rules, behaviors, and strategies into their school routine as daily habits than students in the past. Just telling the students "how" to walk down the hallway or "where" to turn in a paper may not be enough. The teacher needs to model the expected behavior by showing the students *how* to walk down the hallway, *how* to get up from their seats, and *how* to walk over to where they will turn in their paper.

The current situation demands the need for those students to also practice these behaviors in order to maintain them in their regular routines. It is a good idea to have *each* student practice these expected behaviors and routines themselves, not just watch the teacher do it. Teachers should give students praise when they perform the expected behavior correctly. Giving affirmations to the students such as, "You are doing a great job walking down the hallway, Johnny," also assists in solidifying the newly learned behaviors.

This practice seems to be the tool for the "Me" Generation to make the procedures part of their daily routines. With all of the twenty-first century's audiovisual exposure, students have strong auditory skills, but still need to have hands-on experience by actually *acting out* the behavior you are trying to teach. So many times we assume that if we model, the students will understand—and will just do it. But research says that also having the students practice each expected behavior themselves increases their learning.

In addition to learning the regular classroom, hallway, cafeteria, playground, and transition routines, students also need to practice other routines in the school, such as how to come into or behave during morning assemblies or large assembly programs. The expected behavior for these should be practiced as well, so that when it comes time, they will know what to do and have better mastery of the concept.

The toughest challenge for a teacher when implementing a new behavior model is knowing when to use and adjust one's skills and knowledge to meet the demands of the situation. Basing your goals and decisions on a well-developed set of student-centered strategies will assist the school in accomplishing its goals.

Students today very much want to know "why." *Why* do we have to do this? is probably a common question in your classroom. It is an important question to give an important answer to. Students are much like adults: if they understand "why" they are to do something, particularly if they learn that doing so makes sense or helps them in any way, they are more likely to do it.

The Self-Correcting Behavior Modification Model uses methods of teaching this independence and self-management of behavior. Self-management refers to techniques that transfer control of behavior from external reinforcers to the students themselves (Shapiro & Cole 1994). Communication is also an important part of self-management. Children need to know what is expected of them with a clear understanding of behavioral limits.

This leads naturally to a discussion of punishment. Punishment may stop undesired behavior or teach avoidance behavior, but is less effective than positive reinforcement as an adjunct to attaining desired behavioral change. Positive reinforcement may take the form of a reward, such as a treat or a special privilege; but an immediate pat on the back or other acknowledgment can be equally powerful. In setting expectations, teachers, principals, or parents should make them realistic and achievable.

The routines and structure have to be created, communicated, and then taught and re-taught as necessary until they become automatic to the students.

The routines must be efficient, nonnegotiable guidelines for conducting the business of the classroom: How do I walk to the cafeteria? What is expected of me when I come into the classroom after recess or at the beginning of the period? When can I sharpen my pencil? and so forth.

As a teacher or principal, minimize reactions to student's mistakes to extinguish them. When children encounter failure, show them how to correct it and move on, being quick to praise positive results. Remember that practice makes perfect only when the practice is correct. Practicing errors only makes them stronger. When the whole task seems insurmountable, break it down into smaller, more manageable parts. This is sometimes called "chunking" of information.

In the classroom, for example, develop and post a visual agenda every morning, so children know what is expected and can manage their time accordingly. At home, parents can also establish daily routines that are extremely helpful and that can lead to lifelong habits of emotional well-being and productivity. This chapter reinforces how teachers can be a great support to parents with advice on self-management and self-correcting behaviors, expectations, and routines. This alliance and partnership of school and home is crucial to the overall academic success of the children and the ability of educators to provide the best education possible for the students. More examples of model and practice are shared in chapters 8 and 11.

Chapter 8

Using Class Meetings to Build Success

"If teachers are expected to grow professionally and improve their teaching, they must have frequent, insightful, concrete feedback on their performance; opportunities to dialogue about and reflect on the nuances of teaching and learning; meaningful participation in work-study groups focused on improving students' learning; and varied forms of assistance" (Gupton 2003, p. 116).

Chapter 8 discusses how some of these educational reflections and learning moments produce great ideas and strategies for teachers leading to concepts such as class meetings. Many teachers today find it helpful to use class meetings as tool to facilitate an effective collaborative process with their students to assist in ensuring academic success and providing an opportunity for student growth to learn much-needed life skills.

Many theorists and educational authors propose the use of classroom meetings. They believe the process of using class meetings builds a healthy student community and gives them a sense of belonging because they have a place to discuss concerns as well as share about themselves.

WHAT ARE CLASS MEETINGS?

The term *class meetings* can be defined as the simple strategy of setting aside time with students to discuss classroom issues as a group, including such issues as class rules or guidelines, problems students may be having at recess, input on school decisions, and so on. This process allows students to have a voice, to have stakeholder ownership, to learn social skills, and to develop communication and problem-solving skills. This concept also has been noted to improve the overall academics of a student through the process of providing more ownership and a voice in their education.

Class meetings can be valuable multipurpose tools for classrooms of any grade level. They can help to foster a caring environment based on mutual respect and trust, as they allow students to practice democratic processes. Not only can a class meeting work to resolve concerns in the classroom, but it can be useful for the teacher to constantly get a feel for how the students are feeling about the class environment, other students, and themselves.

When to Have Class Meetings

When deciding to utilize class meetings, it is essential for teachers to research and to decide what works best for them. Some teachers have a class meeting every morning before they start the day. Others may have them once a week, or when needed. The meetings usually last about 20–30 minutes. Class meetings help create a sense of community; when students feel their opinions affect the class and them, they are more likely to contribute in a positive manner. A student who misbehaves will be more likely to contribute to the class if he or she is given a "say" in how the class is run.

Sergiovanni (1982) writes about the 10 principles of quality leadership and education including the principle of peopling. The principle of peopling recognizes that very little can happen "without the good wishes of others." Resistance behaviors by their very nature are evidence of the absence of change and learning. The concern we have today as educators is often the speed to which we can impart the necessary changes, as well as having the resources to do so (p. 332).

Class Meetings Are Great for the "Me" Generation!

The process of using class meetings in the classrooms is a perfect idea for the "Me" Generation. This population wants a voice and wants to have more control over their lives and what happens to them. They are also very social and like to work in groups while being able to express their individuality and opinions.

Teachers I have worked with who use the class meeting concept have found that students would like more project-based work and are willing to take homework more seriously if given time at the end of class to work with a partner. Recognition that the class belongs to the students as well as the teacher makes the students more likely to participate in a positive and productive way.

Beth Lewis (2009) with About.com states, "For example, you can hold class meetings to involve students in important decisions such as, How should cheating be handled? or What can we do about teasing in our school? Don't be afraid to let students think about these weighty issues. You may be surprised by the thoughtful and creative solutions your students propose." Lewis promotes the following logic regarding class meetings:

Why have class meetings?

- To get kids involved in constructive decision-making in their classrooms and schools.
- To build a climate of trust and respect between teacher and students, as well as among students.
- To help build self-esteem by getting kids involved in decisions that impact their world in important ways.

Rationale

- Students often develop a better sense of responsibility when given a chance to make meaningful contributions to the world around them.
- When children believe they are contributing to the school environment in a significant way, they feel a more positive attachment to school and are more motivated to learn.
- Students who are allowed to problem solve and make some of their own decisions are likely to buy in to the solutions.

Benefits

- Just as families can use family meetings as times to connect and reflect on their goals and/or problems as a family, class meetings can achieve similar results.
- Class meetings provide children with opportunities for assuming responsibilities.
- Class meetings may help children to take ownership for their actions by involving them in the process of understanding and questioning rules, guidelines, limits, and consequences.
- Children are able to reason/reflect on their actions, think about the consequences of their behavior, and comprehend the impact they have on others.
- Class meetings can help students learn to associate their successes with their own efforts and abilities, thus boosting self-esteem.
- When children feel they are making an important contribution to the world, their motivation and sense of control in their lives can greatly increase.

Donna Styles (2009), author, stated in *Education World*, "I believe that creating community in the classroom and fostering a safe environment in which students are empowered to make choices, provides the rich ground from which confident, self-directed, successful students thrive and grow." Styles, who is experienced in holding both class and family meetings, offers the following tips for successful class meetings:

- Use a formal process, and hold meetings every week
- Use a circle formation, with members sitting in chairs
- Model respectful behavior
- Create a positive classroom environment
- Do not dominate meeting
- Have faith in the creative problem-solving process
- Trust the ability of your students to lead meetings, participate in discussions, choose solutions, and make decisions that will affect the classroom

Rules for Class Meetings

A teacher should establish boundaries for the class meetings, developing rules and guidelines together about "the when and how" of the meeting structure. The teacher acts as a facilitator, providing guidance and keeping the tone positive and helpful, but only speaking at the beginning to start the discussion, and providing guiding questions or responses when assistance is needed.

A technique called "mirroring" can be taught and used in community meetings. Mirroring is a listening technique whereby one student describes a problem, idea, or conflict to another. The second student listens and then repeats, or "mirrors," the first student's thoughts to ensure that the ideas were properly understood. The first student confirms the information is correct; if not, the listening student tries again until it is. If students believe their ideas are respected and valued, they will more likely be productive participants.

When having a class meeting, follow the rules of brainstorming, teaching students the communication skills of how to be respectful, listen, and take turns. Do not accept judgmental tones, remarks, body language, or facial expressions that indicate the ideas are good, bad, or funny. Use others' comments to think of new ideas. Keep discussion of the recorded ideas to a minimum and allow time for an exchange of views later. As a teacher, remember that you hold "veto" power, but use it sparingly for the best results.

Remember the advantages of "Socratic questioning" to help students think through the logic of their proposals. Socratic questioning is a form of inquiry and debate between individuals with opposing viewpoints. Asking and answering questions stimulates critical thinking and illuminates ideas. This process allows students to learn from their mistakes. Let them talk through their ideas, even if you're convinced they won't work, as long as no obvious harm could result.

How Long Should Class Meetings Last?

Allow 20 to 30 minutes for each community meeting. You can record all ideas on a big pad, if you like, so that everyone can see them and so that they can be retrieved at a later date. Encourage all ideas. Offering a sticker to the person with the most ideas or with the most creative suggestion will encourage more ideas and suggestions.

> Class Meetings are the most successful in classrooms that have a warm, caring, supportive environment—classrooms in which students feel comfortable to learn, feel safe to share their ideas, and feel free to ask questions and take risks. Students in those kinds of classrooms are supportive of one another, work together cooperatively, encourage one another, assume responsibility for their own learning and behavior, and are allowed to make decisions. (Styles 2009)

Class Meetings Can Help with Communication and Discipline

Class meetings help make good classrooms even better. The true power of class meetings lies in their ability to empower students, to motivate them to learn, and to help them discover their personal best. When both students and teachers are able to voice opinions and thoughts in a quiet, respectful atmosphere, mutual respect and understanding develop. The students realize that it is *their* classroom as much as the teacher's, and they take ownership and pride in that.

With classroom meetings, discipline seems to become a minor issue. Problems are discussed in meetings, and students themselves determine the consequences for misbehavior. Students become highly accountable for their actions in the classroom when their peers are taking note of their behavior and discussing poor behavior in class meetings. When students choose solutions to problems, they have a stake in seeing that the consequences are followed.

Problems in the classroom are no longer just the teacher's problems to solve; they become the class's problems, even when the students are not in a class meeting. Practice with the process in the class each week enables students to become excellent problem solvers, coming up with fair and effective methods of helping classmates improve and change behaviors that interfere with others or with their learning.

The students using a class suggestion box for ideas allows them an opportunity to give suggestions for the class or interesting and fun activities for the class during the year. This generates excitement and energy in the classroom, helping students to "buy in" to coming to school and to feel a sense of belonging to the group.

As a former teacher, I think there is no other tool that has such a long list of benefits. Conducting weekly class meetings with this format easily makes it one of the most powerful tools a classroom teacher can use. And it's so simple—one period a week! Without exception, students love class meetings—and the approach is conducive to the inclusion of students with special needs.

Chapter 8 discusses how incorporating class meetings can be a reasonable task if teachers prepare students for meetings in two to three lessons during the first weeks of school. The lessons involve the teaching and practice of encouragement and creative problem solving. After several trial meetings with the teacher leading and modeling the process, students can become meeting leaders, with each student taking a turn as discussion leader during the school year. Implementing this process into a classroom makes a significant difference in the management of the classroom and the ability of the teacher to have his or her own form of a professional learning community (PLC) in the classroom. This will inevitably result in a higher-level academic environment for the students as well as a collaborative climate for students.

Chapter 9

Creating a CSI (Critical Strategies Intervention) Classroom Using Technology

"Every day we give a standalone teacher a standalone curriculum, we're recreating this outdated educational model. We need to start thinking about transforming these learning organizations into a twenty-first century learning system," said Tom Carroll (2009), NCTAF president. We need classroom teachers who will inject compelling "real-life" authentic learning lessons into classroom instruction.

"We're living in the learning age," Carroll said. "The standalone teaching model is no longer sustainable, and teachers and students need a collaborative team environment to work in. It is not fair to the teachers or the students." Carroll compared the outdated system of solo teaching to professions that have evolved to incorporate a team-distributed leadership approach, and asked why the nation thinks teachers are the only professionals who should work without teams to assist them.

THE "CSI APPROACH": CRITICAL STRATEGIES INTERVENTION

Many educators and researchers, including myself, are proposing a new kind of collaborative approach to teaching in which educators and students will have supportive team environments to learn in. I call this model the CSI (Critical Strategies Intervention) Approach. This environment is an environment that creates powerful learning for students where they can use their advanced, savvy, technology skills, critical thinking skills, ability to multitask, need for creativity, and need to work in a social group environment that promotes collaboration and socialization while learning.

The rest of the world—for example, the business world—is already creating twenty-first-century learning environments. Teachers need to have focused professional development opportunities to attain the skills and knowledge to be able to create these authentic types of learning environments for the students. Having these skills, information, and strategies allows teachers to organize a learning environment which "mirrors" where these young people live and work in their lives. Providing this "strategic gift of learning" to the students enables them to develop these skills early on and allows them to be more prepared to be a part of today's workforce.

The technology-rich world surrounding schools today makes many powerful resources and network learning opportunities available to students and teachers inside the school prior to graduation. User-driven and user-created content is happening constantly already through such services as Facebook, YouTube, and SecondLife.

CSI Classrooms Use Authentic Learning

Authentic learning is defined as learning that uses real-world problems and projects that allow students to explore and discuss these problems in ways that are relevant to them, such as the learning that occurs in a CSI classroom. Students can work in collaborative groups trying to find the answer "through authentic learning versus the teacher giving them the answer." This kind of learning allows students to use all of their resources and learning styles to find the answer by using multiple strategies and resources.

Lebow (1994) discusses how the authentic learning approach to teaching has students working on realistic problems to gain new knowledge and skills in context, rather than listening to lectures and memorizing vast amounts of information to be reproduced on tests. Students construct their own meanings from their work and produce and generate products and performances that have value or meaning beyond success in school. It is real work, for a real audience.

Authentic learning promotes higher-order thinking and the integration of knowledge rather than strict subject area constraints. It rewards depth of knowledge rather than surface knowledge. It also encourages students who are working alone or in a collegial team to build on ideas connected to the real world.

A CSI Case

A good example of the CSI model is the Jasper Woodbury videodisk series (1993) produced by the Cognition and Technology Group at Vanderbilt University. They provided students with a "macrocontext" for solving authentic problems. The focus of the series is mathematics, but the adventures of Jasper lead to many other areas such as ecology or history. Each video tells a story 14 to 18 minutes long that ends with one of the characters posing a problem. Students then have to consider subtasks and pose possible solutions. In reality, and in the Jasper series, there are many possible solutions to these problems.

It Is Time for a Change

Never has there been a time of greater challenge for education, and never has there been such an opportunity to rethink the whole process. Educators, parents, businesspeople, and other members of the community are asking fundamental questions: What do students need to know, and be able to do, when they graduate? What are the essential academic learning requirements for today—and tomorrow? What kinds of environments, curricula, and educational strategies are appropriate to prepare students for a future that can hardly be imagined?

And other questions such as, How do we reach and teach students from different cultural, social, economic, and educational backgrounds? How can we help students to master basic skills and information, develop understanding and knowledge, and learn to apply what they have learned in contexts outside the classroom? How can we help them to develop the flexible minds and-higher order thinking skills required to live in our rapidly changing world? And are we meeting the needs of all students who have very different ways of learning?

All Students Learn Differently

As educators know from learning about multiple intelligences, students learn differently from each other using a variety of different learning styles. The pioneering split-brain research of Sperry and Bogan (1981) offers new insights into individual differences in learning. Many educators find validation in these studies of what they have always intuitively felt about using different kinds of teaching and learning strategies to reach different kinds of learners.

Younger students in prekindergarten and kindergarten learn through play. Remember when you were that age and it was fun to sing, play, and pretend? You learned while doing so. Children in these grades learn through participation in developmentally appropriate center activities. They learn to develop social skills such as interacting with others in a kitchen center while pretending to make a meal together. They learn problem-solving skills while in a transportation center playing with trucks and learning how to take turns and be safe.

Other types of learning occur through other activities, such as singing while learning the alphabet or other sounds. Having fun and learning at the same time. Some researchers and educators, including myself, are concerned that this is the crucial piece that is missing these days in education. In the absence of sufficient developmental play, students are acting out their stress and frustrations—which then leads to violence.

Dr. Brown, founder of the National Institute for Learning Through Play, calls learning through play *"a fundamental biological process."* He believes it is a major public health issue for students and educators. Educators feel they are under huge pressures to achieve academic excellence these days to the exclusion of having much fun in the classroom.

We Should Listen To Our Brains

Neuroscientists have studied how this information about play might best be applied in the classrooms. They found that playful learning at any age actually leads to better academic success than the skills-and-drills approach does. Educators need to think of new ways of assessing both the potential of students and the learning achievement, such as with the CSI approach with learning through application and authentic learning.

If brain and mind research suggests that everyone can learn, then educators need to understand and have training on how to create environments and use strategies and tools that make this possible. Professional development training should be based on the following questions, among others: What clues does brain research offer to assess potential more effectively? Is the potential evoked through the use of new technologies a useful tool for educators? What are the most important factors to consider in developing the fullest possible potential of students? Are you using differentiated instructional methods in the classroom?

Differentiating instruction and authentic learning are simultaneous and provide different avenues for students to acquire content, process ideas, and develop products to help each student to learn effectively. In all classrooms, teachers deal with at least three curricular elements: (1) *content*, what students learn, (2) *process*, how students make sense of ideas and information, and (3) *product*, how students demonstrate what they learn.

The method of differentiating inspires purposeful movement and exploration, as well as fine-tuning and tailoring of instruction, and must be engaging, interesting, and relevant. This new age of education begins engaging students in "knowing where to find the answer" rather then "knowing what the answer is." Differentiating instruction is about using and knowing what your resources are and how to use them. This authentic learning model teaches students that it is more important to know how to access information than it is to memorize it.

Neuroscientist Engineer (2004) states, "It is no longer believed that the brain stops changing once development is over. Even in adulthood, new connections between neurons are constantly being made, new neurons are being born and brains can reorganize and adapt to novel environments over short time scales."

What can brain studies show us about the differences between students in settings focused on listening, reading, and drill exercises and students who are more actively engaged in multisensory, constructivist learning? There are brain studies of both approaches that show structural and functional change over time; as well as what parts of the brain are most actively involved in the different approaches. A case can be made for using both methods for different purposes in an appropriate balanced classroom approach.

Things Have Changed

In most school systems today, there is a push for higher standards, but there is not always an accompanying effort to equip both students and teachers with the skills to meet them. One concern is that there are increasing high numbers of elementary-age children who were born of mothers who abused drugs, nicotine, and alcohol. There is also the well-known problem of kids' abusing these substances—even at the elementary level. Many of these children do not respond to traditional educational methods, and teachers are desperate for information that will help them and their students.

Many children today are spending inordinate amounts of their free time watching television or playing video games—frequently five or six hours a day—instead of reading or learning. Educators are observing the negative effects of this on students' cognitive, physical, and emotional development, as well as on their interpersonal skills. Brain studies suggest there is a link between the massive use of multimedia technology and short attention spans, the inability to focus the attention.

Violent behavior in schools is also a growing problem. Clearly, there are many reasons, among them environmental and social factors—but evidence is piling up that watching violent TV programs or playing violent video games may cause violent behavior in students, especially in cases in which a student is unstable or already prone to violence.

What happens chemically and functionally in various parts of the brain while watching violent films, playing violent computer games, and interacting with violent websites? In a recent article, Yale psychologist Robert Sternberg (2000) points out that the average intelligence of each generation is rising, not only as measured by I.Q. tests, but also by observing behavior—but also that violence is on the rise with the increase of young students' being exposed to violence and lacking appropriate communication and problem-solving skills.

How We Use Technology as Educators Can Make a Difference

Sternberg suggests that one explanation may lie in the tools educators use, and how we use them—especially new technologies. Brain research says that brain function and higher-order thinking skills will improve by using educationally appropriate, intellectually challenging technologies such as educationally sound Internet sites, Tetris, Lego Logo, the Dr. Brain games (Sierra), and other appropriate educational tools.

The technology of virtual reality is already being used in schools to perform lab experiments, simulate flight, and help children who have learning disabilities. Brain research states that the brain responds differently to virtual reality education, allowing itself to think in three-dimensional, critical-thinking patterns with accelerated learning.

Use of technology, according to research, also increases skill memory, memorization, verbal and visual memory, multitasking skills, problem-solving skills, and creativity. Some years ago, Herman Epstein (1967) studied brain-growth spurts and plateau periods. He suggested that periods of rapid brain growth are the times for intellectually challenging curriculum, and that plateau periods, such as adolescence, are the times for more concrete, experiential learning rather than pushing students too soon into abstract thinking.

Education is changing, and our teaching needs to change, too. In this twenty-first-century society, students are digital natives. They have grown up surrounded by technology as an integral part of everyday life and are comfortable "speaking the language."

Our students have changed radically. Therefore, we need to shift our way of thinking about school to a twenty-first-century model and reflect upon our daily educational practices. We need to apply a student-centered approach in which learning is achieved through students' engagement in motivating and authentic learning activities.

Author Carol Tomlinson (2001) states, "In a differentiated classroom, commonalities are acknowledged and built upon, and student differences become important elements in teaching and learning as well." Students have multiple opportunities for taking in information, making sense of ideas, and expressing what they learn.

Teachers are learning to do more with less in our current economical situation. Students are using less paper and more hands-on authentic learning centers, using computers, the Internet, cell phones, and iPods, as well as real-world experiences.

Prensky (2009) shared that the average cell phone now has more computing power than many of the computers of 10 years ago. Below are some ideas of how to use cell phones in classroom instruction:

10 Ideas for Using Cell Phones in Education

1. Student response polling or pop quizzes (no need to invest in additional devices).
2. Use SMS (Short Message Service) to send texts, connect to the Internet, etc., to find definitions, currency conversion, math equations, translations, and more.
3. Use as an Internet browser to access endless information.
4. Research.
5. Read news articles and current events.
6. Read books.
7. Download and use education programs such as Google Maps to use as a GPS.
8. Use as a digital or video camera to accompany school projects, publishing, and so on.
9. Educate students on appropriate and acceptable social use of cell phones.
10. Use voice technology to share engaging lectures or lessons.

Critical Strategies Intervention Strategies for the "Me" Generation

The "Me" Generation has a lot of gifts and a lot of baggage. They are an intelligent group but are hard to handle. Educators need to formulate lesson plans that constantly challenge these young Einsteins with critical stimulus intervention strategies.

Rockman (1995) suggested that teachers can use some of the suggested strategies below to guide them in creating technology-based, authentic learning experiences for their students:

- Work with your students to identify meaningful projects within your school's curriculum framework. Help students focus on large concepts and guide them toward determining appropriate outcomes for each project.
- Encourage and accept student autonomy and initiative. Students are motivated by taking responsibility for their own learning and by constructing knowledge based on their own ideas.

- Have students work with raw data and primary sources along with manipulative, interactive, and physical materials. Learning becomes more meaningful to students as they make connections during the process of gathering, analyzing, and drawing conclusions about information.
- Once a task is chosen and students determine what resources they need, encourage contact with the larger community by letter, telephone, fax, and electronic communications such as online services and the Internet. Technology-based research can be specialized and current, and enables students to obtain resources outside the school network.
- Have students make use of technology for data collection, information management, problem-solving, decision-making, communications, and presentations. For example, science students performing hands-on investigations can use technology-based tools such as database search programs, spreadsheets, and graphing software to help them integrate and synthesize information. For a project on the stock market, students can collect information from an online service and use a database to organize it. E-mail enables students to work collaboratively with peers in other locations to write and assemble the pieces of a multimedia presentation.
- Be alert for opportunities to introduce experiences that might contradict initial hypotheses; students learn as they engage in resolving discrepancies. Move toward high-order thinking skills by guiding students to technology-based tools to classify, analyze, predict, or create.

Chapter 9 discusses how important it is to provide a daily, stimulus-rich learning environment in the classroom with the use of critical intervention strategies through methods such as learning through play, differentiated instruction, and authentic learning. More and more educators are starting to realize that neuroscience research can contribute to understanding why learning environments are so important for building healthy brains. These results confirm most teachers' intuition that the rich, stimulating environments they provide really do make a difference, and indicate that boring, stale environments may actually have negative consequences on the brain, as well as causing student behavior problems and teacher burnout.

Fun and exciting class lessons provide "real-world education" that prepares students for college and the work world, that gets them interested and excited about learning, and that embraces authentic learning and the use of their technology skills in their daily learning.

Chapter 10

Modeling as a Leader

A friend once told me, "It is not how far you fall, but how you bounce when you get there." This is probably a really good description of "the life of a leader." Being a leader is one of the hardest jobs—if not the hardest job—out there. Many people go into the leadership field to be a principal or superintendent because they want to make a difference, just as teachers do. They want to lead a good team to the boundaries of academic success and have a high-performing school or district. Leaders know they cannot do it alone, so they look for a school or district that is on the right track and a good team of staff who are all going in the same direction, sharing the same goals and mission.

The twenty-first century is probably the hardest time to be a leader. Schools have lots of challenges, including the floundering economy, lack of funding for schools, the pressures that come with teaching, the accountability pressure of NCLB, the high number of discipline problems and violence that afflict students, and everything else that is going on with society and the "Me" Generation. It is almost impossible to get everything done in a manageable amount of time; the work seems overwhelming most days.

Many educational leaders have implemented models such as professional learning communities (PLCs) to empower their staff to share in leadership. PLCs are defined as extended learning opportunities to foster collaborative learning among colleagues within a particular work environment or field, and are often used in schools as a way to organize teachers into working groups. Different variations of PLCs exist and include collaborating classroom practice in the school community, bringing community personnel into the school to enhance the curriculum and learning tasks for students, and engaging students, teachers, and administrators simultaneously in learning.

Richard Dufour, a recognized national expert in PLCs, believes that to create a professional learning community, the focus needs to be on learning first and teaching second, working collaboratively with the entire school community—which includes parents—using the results and holding oneself accountable for the results. This model of a shared vision or running a school is one in which everyone can make a contribution, and in which staff are encouraged to collectively undertake activities and reflection in order to constantly improve students' performance. The idea behind a PLC is to integrate two concepts that in the past have been quite distinctive from each other: professionalism and community.

Educational leaders are aware that many teachers and other educators often feel as if they are pawns in a larger game of chess in which school and district leaders place obstacles to educators doing their jobs. Such feelings can inhibit the ideas and development from administrators of collaborative programs such as PLCs. If teachers could only walk in an administrator's shoes for one day, they would find the view much different from what they currently envision it to be.

With the current challenges for schools in mind, leaders want to establish a system that works. Establishing an effective staff development team approach and a powerful strategy for school change and possible improvement is the only hope for our schools today. The mission should be a reflective process where both individual and school community growth is achieved. Among the team there must be a shared vision of where they want the school to be.

In his book *The Fifth Discipline*, Peter Senge comments on shared vision and states, "The practice of shared vision involves the skills of unearthing shared 'pictures of the future' that foster genuine commitment and enrollment rather than compliance." This type of collaborative effort may seem hard, at first, to organize and keep going, but with communication, teamwork, and a systematic approach, the effort will be worth it. Through this commitment and creation of a shared vision, the team, including leaders, participants, and staff, becomes empowered to work together to attain their goals.

Educational leaders get excited about the possibilities when using this collaborative model. Under this model, many things can happen. A team concept is always much stronger than an individual concept and can do much, much more. Teaching strategies such as the use of authentic instruction, reflective learning, inquiry-based learning, constructivist learning, and Critical Strategies Intervention (CSI) techniques, when used collaboratively, increase student achievement and teacher empowerment—and the results can be tremendous.

The benefits of programs such as professional learning communities to educators and students include reduced isolation of teachers, better-informed and more committed teachers, and academic gains for students. Educational expert Michael Fullan states that programs such as PLCs are necessary: "Numerous studies document the fact that professional learning communities or collaborative work cultures at the school and ideally at the district level are critical for the implementation of attempted reforms."

The emphasis of these collaborative team programs is on emphasizing and improving student learning, shared values and norms, and development of common practices and feedback. Dufour and Eaker (1998) and Levine and Shapiro (2004), as cited in *Education for All*, further break down these points and indicate the characteristics of programs such as PLCs:

- Shared vision and values that lead to a collective commitment of school staff, expressed in day-to-day practices
- Solutions actively sought; openness to new ideas
- Working teams cooperate to achieve common goals
- Encouragement of experimentation as an opportunity to learn
- Questioning of the status quo, leading to an ongoing quest for improvement and professional learning
- Continuous improvement based on evaluation of outcomes rather than intentions expressed
- Reflection in order to study the operation and impacts of actions taken

If schools are to be significantly more effective, they must break from the industrial model upon which they were created and embrace a new model that enables them to function as collaborative learning organizations. The idea that there is one main decision-maker who controls the organization is not sufficient in today's school. All people within the school community must work effectively toward common goals. Although individuals are responsible for their own actions, feelings, and opinions, it is the common good of the community that guides the decision-making.

It is important for leadership in the schools to establish and maintain a collaborative working model with the staff. Successful PLCs require a shift in the traditional leadership role from a leader-centered (top-down) to shared leadership. Educational leaders must be willing to do this, and buy in this process, in order for the school to be successful as an academic organization.

Often, a top-down leader creates the vision statement; staff members are then encouraged to adhere to the goals outlined in the statement. But this is not how PLCs work. There must be staff buy-in and ownership for these programs to work. Many times educators feel that new ideas coming from someone else without teacher input are a waste of time and do not qualify as true leadership or support. Principals need to lead from the center rather than the top.

Chapter 10 verifies how the view of the principal as the instructional leader is changing to one that reflects the principal's role within a community of learners and leaders. The practice of shared vision involves the skills of unearthing shared "pictures of the future" that foster genuine commitment and enrollment rather than compliance. In mastering this discipline, leaders learn the counterproductiveness of trying to dictate a vision, no matter how heartfelt. Through this commitment and creation of a shared vision, the team is empowered to work together and achieve goals. Top-down mandates and bottom-up energies need each other. This process involves sharing diverse ideas and making compromises so that all people are satisfied with the direction in which the school is moving. As teachers' capacity increases and they develop a feeling of success, they will better understand that when they ally their strengths and skills, they are able to reach goals they could not reach on their own.

Chapter 11

Practice during Recess

A school has many important parts to it, such as the classroom, school activities, recess, lunch, and so forth. This chapter discusses how recess or lunch time is a period that can be a management task for school personnel, like other areas such as classroom management or hallway management. There are lots of thoughts and opinions out there about the role of recess and lunch time in the learning and development of children and students. It has been a given for a long time that recess and lunch time are just part of a school's schedule.

Recess or lunch is probably one of the most favorite times of the students. They have a chance to run and play, talk, and visit with their friends. A long time ago, boys and girls were separated and had to play in different areas of the playground. Some schools still separate grade levels into different areas.

Historically, "breaks" besides recess were taken during the school day to allow children to have that natural play time and social time to learn how to play with others. Such breaks were given to factory workers years ago, arising from the belief that after a reasonable amount of work, a person needs a break.

This is similar to what China does with its students and schools. Many schools in China begin school at 7:30 a.m. and take a break from 11:00 a.m. to 1:00 or 1:30 p.m. Elementary students go home from school at 5:30 p.m.; secondary students break from 5:30 p.m. to 7:00 p.m. and then return until 9:00 p.m.—if doing independent studies, until 11:00 p.m. The Chinese believe these breaks help students to be more productive in the long run, similar to taking a "siesta" in the Mexican culture. Pellegrini and Davis (1993) believe that prolonged periods of confinement in classrooms have been found to lead to increased fidgeting, restlessness, and the subsequent inability to concentrate for students.

It may be helpful for adults to step back and reflect on the break periods that are an important part of our day. Just as judges and lawyers take a recess during court sessions and office workers take breaks during the day to relax and recharge, children also need a time for recess. This may mean that educators and parents need to reexamine the valuable experiences that take place outside of the classroom and compromise between what is developmentally and academically important for children.

Anthony Pellegrini (2005) makes the comparison of working on an assembly line for a long time or taking a long trip: The longer you drive, the less attentive and safe you are. The driver must pull over, take a rest, and start again, more attentive and safer. Pellegrini relates this theory to what current laws dictate for commercial truck drivers and airline pilots. Commercial truck drivers and airline pilots can only drive for a certain period of time—logging their hours—before they must take a break in the spirit of being "safe and attentive."

Movements over the years to "get rid of recess" have sprung up, stating that recess is a waste of valuable time that could be used as instructional time. Some parents have used the argument that recess is just a time for children to be bullied. At one point, Atlanta public schools replaced recess with physical education classes. Although the time periods for recesses or breaks have been minimized in some school districts, there is still at least one recess—the one attached to a lunch period for students. Could this be part of the reason why schools are having so many discipline problems?

Recently, mandates passed in certain states to have "organized recess." This movement came out of the crisis related to childhood diabetes that seems to currently be a problem in the United States. In numerous controlled studies, it is documented that children's attention to school tasks decreased the longer they were deprived of a break, and that children were significantly more attentive after a break than before. The Council on Physical Education for Children (2001) has publically stated its belief that recess is a necessary natural development strategy for children in school and crucial to their learning and development.

Recess is viewed as a venue to the social development of a child. Play is perceived as a way for children to improve their cognitive skills, language skills, and ability to focus on learning and social and emotional development by allowing children to practice life skills such as conflict resolution, cooperation, sharing, and problem solving (Steinhagen & Iltus 2004; Clements 2001; NAECDS/SDE 2001; Jambor 1999).

Pre-kindergarten programs use the learning model of "learning through play" with the belief that play is developmentally appropriate for that age of children. A study published in the February 2009 edition of the *Journal of Pediatrics* (Pope 2009) studied the links between recess and classroom behavior among 11,000 children ages 8 and 9. The study shows those students having more than 15 minutes of recess a day had better behavior in class than those who had little or no recess.

Although studies have shown that disadvantaged children are more likely to be denied recess, the association between bad behavior and recess time held up, even after researchers controlled a number of variables, including sex, ethnicity, public or private school, and class size. Herb Wong, author, believes that recess is not just a break or a rest time, but a learning opportunity time that is just as important, developmentally, as classroom time. Wong (2007) states that "[t]he intensity of play and the range of play behaviors have increased, providing opportunities to develop important lessons on cooperation, ownership, belonging, respect, and responsibility."

School grounds are being increasingly recognized as an integral and valued component of the learning environment. As more research is undertaken, perhaps in time the schoolyard will be seen as a place where the formal education curriculum can be supported alongside the equally valued informal learning that occurs in the playground environment.

Although educators agree that recess is important and necessary for the overall development of a child, many educators and parents worry about the "rough play" that is seen on school campuses these days. Students hitting, kicking, biting, punching, bullying, and so on have replaced simple disagreements. Sometimes the playground witnesses violent acts where someone gets badly hurt, sometimes by someone using a weapon.

Teachers and principals have noticed the increase in playground problems along with the increase in discipline in the classrooms. It seems that sitting students "out" on the sidewalk or on the bench, giving them detention, and suspending them for fighting are not necessarily working to change observed problem behavior.

Educators can benefit from using the same Self-Correcting Behavior Modification Model approach and practice on the playground. When a teacher on duty sees a student exhibiting inappropriate behavior, the student should be called over to discuss the situation with the teacher while focusing only on the behavior, and not the personhood. The teacher should address the problem behavior and discuss with the student why the student thinks (or does not think) the behavior is a problem, and how the behavior should be different.

The student then stays with the teacher for a few minutes and continues to discuss what appropriate behavior looks like, by having the student identify other students' behavior on the playground that is appropriate. Once the student feels that he or she knows what the appropriate behavior looks like, and what it should be, the teacher can send the student back out to the playground to have a chance to practice the appropriate behavior.

Susan Ohanian (2003), author and the 2003 National Teacher of the Year, talks about "keeping one foot in the chicken coop and keeping an eye on what really counts." If a method isn't working, why are we still doing it? This is one of the factors stressing out our teachers and administrators. The old methods of behavior management are not working with the "Me" Generation, so it is time to change to a new method that will work, such as the Self-Correcting Behavior Modification Model.

This chapter emphasizes how the students are sometimes just exhibiting the behaviors they display at home, not realizing that they are doing something wrong. Many of the students coming into the schools today are lacking appropriate communication skills, social skills, and problem solving skills. Educators who have been around for a while may feel as if this is déjà vu, but as they say, everything cycles in education. It is time to get back to the basics. Teachers cannot teach the students if they are doing discipline all of the time. Teaching students appropriate communication skills and problem solving skills helps them in school, especially during recess, the most physical time of day for the students. It will also decrease the number of discipline referrals.

Chapter 12

Working with Parents

"A strong and growing body of evidence clearly shows that students learn better when the major forces in their lives—family, school, and community—work together" (NCTAF 2009). Principals and teachers should always strive to build and maintain positive relations with parents and the community. The Business Roundtable's *Essential Components of a Successful Education System* (2009) addresses the nine essential components for a school district while pointing out the importance of parent involvement in the schools.

1. *Standards:* A successful system clearly defines, in measurable terms, expectations for what students need to know and be able to do to succeed in school, in the workplace, and in life. A successful system aligns and focuses its policies and programs on student achievement of high academic standards.
2. *Assessments:* A successful system focuses on results, measuring and reporting student, school, and system performance so that students, teachers, parents, and the public can understand and act on the information.
3. *Accountability:* A successful system bases consequences for policymakers, educators, and students on demonstrated performance. It provides students the curriculum, instruction, and time they need to succeed. It assists schools that are struggling to improve, rewards exemplary schools, and penalizes schools that persistently fail to educate their students.
4. *Professional Development:* A successful system insists on meaningful preparation and continuous learning for teachers and administrators that drives improved teaching, learning, and school management.
5. *School Autonomy:* A successful system gives individual schools the freedom of action and resources necessary for high performance and true accountability.

6. *Parent Involvement:* A successful system enables parents to support the learning process, influence schools, and make choices about their children's education.
7. *Learning Readiness:* A successful system recognizes the importance of the years before children come to school. It provides high-quality prekindergarten for disadvantaged children. It also seeks the help of other public and private agencies to overcome learning barriers caused by poverty, neglect, violence, or ill health for students of all ages.
8. *Technology:* A successful system uses technology to broaden access to knowledge and to improve learning and productivity.
9. *Safety and Discipline:* A successful system provides a safe, well-disciplined, caring environment for student learning.

A SUCCESSFUL SCHOOL SYSTEM

A successful school system enables a climate where parents can support the learning process, can influence schools and students with their participation, and are involved and make choices about their children's education. Joyce Epstein (1995, p. 173), author of the *Six Types of Parent Involvements*, discusses how "[t]here are many reasons for developing school, family, and community partnerships. The main reason to create such partnerships is to help all youngsters succeed in school and in later life."

The strongest and most consistent predictors of parent involvement at school and at home are the specific school programs and teacher practices that encourage parent involvement at school and guide parents in how to help their children at home. School-initiated activities to help parents learn how to specifically help their children with academics can have a strong influence on children's school performance.

Lack of parental involvement is the biggest problem facing public schools today. The earlier in a child's educational process parent involvement begins, the more powerful the effects.

In today's times, it is important to remember that there are a lot of grandparents raising grandchildren who need the same type of support as parents. Research says that 86% of the general public believes that support from parents and other parental figures, such as grandparents, is the most important way to improve the schools.

Although most parents and guardians do not know how to help their children with their education; with guidance and support from a teacher, counselor, principal, or even mental health counselor, parents can become increasingly involved in school activities. By helping their children with homework and projects, or through in-home learning activities to continue the enrichment of learning with weekend trips to the zoo or a museum, for example, parents find themselves with opportunities to teach, to be models for, and to guide their children.

The most effective forms of parent involvement are those that engage parents in working directly with their children on learning activities at home. Epstein's (1995) research discusses how family participation in education is twice as predictive of students' academic success as the family's socioeconomic status. Meaning, despite the economic status of the parent, the more intensely parents of an economic status are involved, the more beneficial the achievement effects for the child.

Parent Involvement Can Make a Big Difference

In addition to helping their own children, some parents participate in schools at every level. This includes participating in advocacy and on committees, filling decision making and oversight roles, holding fund-raisers and running booster clubs, joining parent/teacher organizations, acting as crosswalk guards and recess and cafeteria monitors, offering services as volunteers and para-professionals, volunteering as homeroom parents, and being at-home teachers by continuing educational support at home.

Schools have helped a lot of parents learn how to help their children by learning how to read and build comprehension and how to help with homework by providing resources, including lessons during parent/teacher conferences, mock presentations, parent workshops, and so on. Giving parents specific information about how to help their children can make a big difference in the child's learning and retention skills.

How to Help My Child Read and Learn

Ask your child, "What do you think the book is about?" as you show him or her the cover and flip through the book before reading it. When schools encourage children to practice reading at home with parents, children make significant gains in reading achievement when compared to those who only practice at school.

It is not just about reading to your child or having him or her read to you anymore. It is important to teach parents *how* to read to children by using such methods as asking them *Who, What, Where, When,* and *How* at the end of every page to build comprehension. Do a picture walk and discuss the vocabulary while flipping through the book to pique the interest of your child before you begin reading. Encourage reading and writing, and have discussions about books and literature with the entire family.

Many parents want to be a part of their child's education and extend the learning into their homes by having books available at home, taking trips, guiding television watching, and providing other kinds of stimulating experiences that contribute to student achievement. The most consistent predictors of children's academic achievement and social adjustment are parental expectations of the child's academic attainment and satisfaction with their child's education at school.

The extent to which parents believe that they can have a positive influence on their children's education depends upon a parent's comfort and perception of his or her own abilities in being able to help and provide educational opportunities for his or her children. This includes parental perceptions that the child and the school want him or her to be involved.

Most students at all levels—elementary, middle, and secondary—want their families to be more knowledgeable partners about schooling and are willing to take active roles in assisting communications between home and school. When parents come to school regularly, it reinforces the view in the child's mind that school and home are connected, and that school is an integral part of the whole family's life.

Research says that families whose children are doing well in school exhibit certain characteristics. They establish a daily family routine and provide time and a quiet place for their child to study. They set aside time to help their children with their homework. They assign responsibilities to the child for household chores, are consistent about bedtime, and have dinner together at the table.

This may seem inconsequential, but is very important to help your child. Learning to be responsible and follow rules will help the child to do the same at school while being able to sit still, follow directions, be respectful, and be focused, as well as having less discipline problems.

Setting limits on television watching, or turning off the television so your child can do his or her homework or study, checking on your child when you are not home, and arranging for after-school activities and supervised care are other characteristics that research shows can make a difference in your child's learning, helping your child feel safe, and have less distractions. Parents need to be clear to supervised caregivers of what kind of care and educational assistance you want from them: for example, the children should begin working on their homework at 4:00 p.m., after a snack and a few minutes of playtime.

Parents who model the value of learning, self-discipline, and hard work can also make a big difference. They can communicate with their child through questioning and conversation, demonstrating that achievement comes from working hard. Asking open questions such as, "Tell me what you learned in math today," "Tell me one thing you liked about your social studies lesson today," "What was your favorite class activity today?" and so forth, rather than just asking, "How was school today?" allows the parent to get specific answers, not just "Fine."

Maintaining a warm, supportive, and safe home, showing your interest in your children's progress at school by asking open-ended questions and displaying and sharing their work, and helping your children with their homework shows your children that you care.

It is fun and exciting to discuss the value of a good education and possible career options with your child. Taking them to visit colleges or enrolling them in "Kid's College" during the summer continues academic and developmental growth while introducing them to new opportunities.

Parents need to express high but realistic expectations for achievement. Setting age-appropriate goals and standards for the children's age and maturity, recognizing and encouraging their special talents, and informing and involving friends and family about your children's successes, encourages your child to continue doing well. Remember, grandmothers love to get a pretty picture in the mail or a copy of the math paper on which a student made an A.

Parents of high-achieving students tend to set higher standards for their children's educational activities than parents of low-achieving students. Decades of research show that when parents are involved, students have

- Higher grades, test scores, and graduation rates
- Better school attendance
- Increased motivation, better self-esteem
- Lower rates of suspension
- Decreased use of drugs and alcohol
- Fewer instances of violent behavior

Recruiting Parents' Help

It is important that parents stay in touch with their child's teachers and school staff and be visible at the school, including by visiting classes and going on educational field trips. Parents need specific information on how to assist and what to do in a school if the school or teacher is trying to recruit help. Parents are very busy these days, with both parents usually working, or with a working single parent, and need to know specifically what the teacher or school needs, and when.

Teachers, principals, and the PTA or PTO should be very specific when asking for help: "I need your help from noon to 1:00 p.m. on Wednesdays to stuff Thursday folders," or "I need you to bring snacks for the first week of each month," or "I need your help this Thursday night at 6:00 p.m. to help set up for the prom," and so forth.

Just asking for volunteers on a sign-up list at Back-to-School Night will only gather contact information and give you a list out of which seven out of eight parents, when called, may not be able to help. The best method is a personal phone call with a follow-up note. Some parents prefer an e-mail or a text; other parents prefer a letter in the mail, a note sent home with their child, or a phone call.

How is it best to communicate with parents with other school matters? Inform parents at the beginning of the year what your routine will be in terms of communication. Have a form to let parents know if you have a Weekly Newsletter or folder that goes home, if you use your school homepage, a blog, MySpace, or so on.

Parents need to know what to expect, what the routine is, what is coming up in terms of school activities, and how to get in contact with you as well. Design effective forms of school-to-home and home-to-school communications about school programs and children's progress. Sometimes, these are simple smiley-face-type forms on which you can just circle and write a short note to the parent, or on which the child can write a note to the parent about how good his or her day was.

As a continued support, if needed, you can work with the parent and have a sticker chart on the refrigerator at home. If the child gets a smiley face that day or each day that week, he or she gets a sticker on the refrigerator chart and can have a treat or extra time on a video game (for example). You can modify this system based on the age of the child.

Research shows that parent attendance and involvement in schools decline with each grade level, and drop dramatically at the transition to middle grade, and then again at the high school level.

Educators often think that low-income parents and single parents will not or cannot spend as much time helping their children at home as do middle-class parents who have more education and leisure time. This is not necessarily true. Really good, hard-working single or low-income parents work at home with their children, attend parent/teacher conferences, and help out at the school as well. The key is to recruit, recruit, recruit all parents!

Community-Wide Partnership Schools

With the continued look at supporting schools and parents, some schools took a strong belief of merging community support efforts with the school system called Community-Wide Partnership Schools. School districts around the country, such as Tulsa Public Schools (2010) in Tulsa, Oklahoma, have begun Community-Wide Partnership Schools that have a network of family support city offices right in the school, including

- Positive early childhood care and development
- Health/health education
- Mental health/social services
- Family/community engagement
- Youth development/out-of-school time
- Neighborhood development
- Life-long learning

These types of programs can offer services such as Head Start Three-Year-Old programs, the Department of Social/Human Services, outside counseling services, legal assistance with an officer on site, a nurse who can give assistance on health and nutrition to the families, English Language classes for parents, and so forth. It is a one-stop type of shop model for parents.

Tulsa Public Schools (2010) believe that this is very convenient, and that it provides a great deal of support for their parents and community. It is both a place and a network of supportive partnerships between the school and the community, promoting improved student learning, stronger families, and healthier communities. It is just another way of supporting parents and making education a daily part of their lives.

This chapter reinforces how building a community and working collaboratively in support for the families will help schools and educators continue to be able to provide for the multiple needs of student populations, and will help the educational staff do a comprehensive job, with support, remaining in the educational field and in the classrooms.

Chapter 13

Stabilizing and Maintaining a Consistent Environment

It is said that significant, lasting change must come from within people and organizations. The word *accountability* is used a lot in education these days. Is this really the word we should be using when looking at education? Maybe we should put more focus on teaching, professional development, and consistency. So much time in education is spent on testing and giving assessments that many teachers feel that they do not have time to teach. Chapter 13 discusses the importance of establishing and maintaining a consistent environment in a school.

Most educators do think there is a purpose to, and need for, assessments that gauge where the students are that drive instruction, but it seems that that is all that we do. In 2009, when President Obama began discussing the reform of No Child Left Behind and even the possible changing of the name, I couldn't help but think about a new name. Maybe we should change the name to "Teach Every Child," putting the focus back on teaching. After all, isn't that why we are here?

We are losing many good teachers, principals, and superintendents due to the stress and pressure in the schools with the accountability movement. Somewhere, there has to be a middle ground that includes appropriate assessment, such as a growth model, but that still allows for teaching.

GROWTH MODEL

A growth model would allow for the assessment of a child's individual growth and could replace the state testing and nine-week benchmark assessments, doing away with much testing. This is a perfect model to use in today's times with the different populations we have and the amount of mobility that our families have. This would be a welcome change that educators would embrace.

As a continued practice, our onsite educational leaders will continue to guide teachers to use the testing data to not only help our students, but to also use the data results to make sure that educators are constantly reflecting and growing as professionals. This will provide a stable and consistent focus on the overall educational plan, mission, and vision in our schools. If we don't know where we are going, how will we know when we have arrived?

The statement "start with the end in mind" probably rings a familiar bell, especially if someone has been on strategic planning committees in a school. If a school has a clear focus of where it wants to be, it is much easier to develop a plan of how to get there.

An investment commercial recently stated that the biggest investment you have is "your people." So true! Hire good people, be on the same page with the same mission, keep those good people, support them, and you will have success. Collaboration is a crucial part of success in schools today.

The Power of Collaboration

Teachers enjoy the chance to collaborate, and that process cannot be emphasized enough in education today. This is where many teachers continue to grow and learn. A strong focus and commitment on professional development in strategies teaching teachers and principals "how to" and about teacher collaboration is very beneficial to educators. The power for teachers is not only being a good teacher, but having a good team to work with.

Does the administration have each grade or subject level's plan time scheduled at the same time so that the teachers can collaborate and work together? If not, how can the administration make that happen? Do the teachers know how to utilize their team time effectively? Schools will have a higher rate of teacher retention if these types of questions are answered and are in place. The job of educating students in the twenty-first century is far too complex to successfully attempt it alone.

In order to be successful and high-performing, administrators have to be very clear about their expectations from the teachers about quality teaching and meeting the criteria and standards. They must evaluate the teachers based on producing these expectations.

Students' educational experiences should be personalized. The instruction should be tailored to the student's needs, and a growth model assessment should be used to complement and accurately analyze each individual student's work and abilities.

Many people have seen the television show *CSI* (*Crime Scene Investigation*). The show models an example of how you can take different people with different strengths and skills and work together on a project as an individual and a team to solve a problem or find a solution. This is a model of inquiry-based learning. Kids love it! This model should be used more in the classrooms.

These students today are very bright and want to work in this kind of environment. They want to be challenged, and they would love to do the intensive research to find answers. All we have to do as a school is to provide the atmosphere, the equipment, and the instruction and direction to do so. Easy as pie, right? So, why are we not doing it?

We have seen little pockets of teaching done this way, but just imagine how successful we could be if we used this method in every subject area that is taught! We would have students who were very interested in instruction, students learning new skills and strengthening the skills they have, students having ownership in their education, teachers who love their jobs, higher test scores, and less discipline issues, and we would retain more good teachers and principals in our buildings and schools.

Student-Led Conferencing

Another way to allow students to have ownership is with student-led conferencing. Parents and teachers love to do student-led conferencing in schools! In this process, students build a portfolio, which shows their progress as they are learning, and then the student actually conducts the conference and tells the parents what and how much he or she has learned.

This is a great way to build ownership into the education of the students. Students are usually very proud to tell their parents how much they have learned. You will see the maturity level raised as if the student was trying to sell himself or herself in a job interview, as well as seeing the pride in the parent as he or she listens and watches the student explain what he or she is learning.

Keefe and Jenkins (2002) believe that "personalized instruction reflects deep concerns for learners and the willingness to search for ways to adjust the teaching and learning environment to meet the learning needs of individual students" (p. 440).

In her book *The Instructional Leadership Toolbox*, Sandra Gupton (2003) discusses how a special section in the February 2002 issue of *Phi Delta Kappan* was devoted to personalized educational instruction. James Keefe and John Jenkins describe how two schools (Thomas Haney Secondary Centre in Maple Ridge, British Columbia, and Francis W. Parker Charter Essential School in Devens, Massachusetts) do so using their own unique learner-centered approaches, such as examples of a dual teacher role of coach and advisor, diagnosis of relevant student learning characteristics, a collegial school culture, an interactive school environment, flexible scheduling and pacing, and use of an authentic assessment model (p. 450).

Ornstein (1993) believes that, "The most effective teachers endow their students with a "can do" attitude, with good feelings about themselves that are indirectly and eventually related to cognitive achievement . . . We're wrong to insist that all teachers must use certain methods and procedures. Instead, we must permit teachers to teach according to their own personalities, teaching philosophies, and goals . . . Although research on teacher competencies offers insight into good teaching, it can lead us to become too rigid in our view of effective teaching" (p. 27). Change begins with a new way of thinking.

How the Economy Affects Schools and Children

Want to know what the true lasting impact of this great recession will be? Then take a look at the kids, according to an economic insight and analysis from *The Wall Street Journal* (2009). A parent's job loss increases the probability that a child repeats a grade in school by roughly 15 percent, according to a new paper from two economics professors at the University of California–Davis.

"If we view grade repetition as a signal of academic difficulties, these short-run effects may be consistent with findings of longer-term negative outcomes in education and earnings," write Ann Huff Stevens and Jessamyn Schaller (2009). The effects are particularly large for families in which the parents have only a high school education or less, their study finds.

"This is in contrast to earlier work that has found only limited evidence of short-run effects of displacement on children's academic outcomes," Stevens and Schaller stated. Their study may also explain why areas of the country that are prone to cyclical layoffs, such as those with a large factory base, have trouble improving their school systems due to families moving around to find work.

In these studies, household earnings are reduced by about 15 percent in the year after a parent's job loss, based on their analysis of data from the Survey of Income and Program Participation (SIPP) in 1996, 2001, and 2004, a program maintained by the Census Bureau. In turn, while just over 7 percent of children without a parental layoff repeated grades by the third SIPP study, more than 9 percent of children who had a parent laid off repeated grades, resulting in about a 15 percent greater chance that children who experience a parent's job loss will repeat a grade. The studies also concluded that the effect is twice as likely in boys as in girls.

The findings come as the nation's unemployment rate hit 10.2 percent in October 2009; the first time it has crossed double digits since 1982. A broader gauge of unemployment, including those who are working part-time for lack of full-time work, is at 17.5 percent. According to the Labor Department, about 15.7 million Americans are currently unemployed.

"More attention should be paid to the potential role of external factors in affecting school level outcomes. Schools in areas with large concentrations of displaced workers . . . may face particular challenges in maintaining achievement standards during times of economic hardship," Stevens and Schaller conclude.

This is important information for schools to keep in mind as we continue in our current economic situation and how it may affect our students, staff, parents, and schools. It seems that stress is a constant factor with parents and students and, inadvertently, affects the school staff. Is it affecting the learning of our students? You bet! How many people do you know who can learn well under distress?

Learning Challenges

Research shows that more and more students are reading below grade level, being retained, and being tested for special education. Ricky is one of many who struggle in school. He is a sixth-grader with a brilliant imagination and advanced language skills, but he cannot write. That's because he has trouble handling spelling, punctuation, grammar, letter formations, and facts all at once with a sheet of paper in front of him. Adults call him lazy, and he is fast becoming a "bad" boy. His family moves around often, making it even more difficult for him to excel and learn. Then there's Beth, a bright girl who gets baffled by sequences of anything, multi-step instructions or math problems—even presenting her ideas when she talks or writes. Her classmate Wendy is an effervescent red-haired girl of many talents who nevertheless endures constant frustration because she has serious problems remembering what she has read, even though she can understand the content quite well. As she puts it, "Whenever I read, each sentence erases the one that went before it."

These are examples of children with normal or superior overall cognitive ability who are contending with differences in the wiring of their brains, subtle but important neurodevelopmental variations that impede their learning productivity and enjoyment of education.

In addition to deficiencies in basic skills such as reading, writing, or mathematics, some of the manifestations are less obvious. The students may have difficulties managing time, expressing ideas in language, remembering facts or problem-solving methods on a test, understanding key concepts, or gaining social acceptance from peers.

What's common between them, however, is that these struggling kids are often misunderstood and affected by the adult world. Learning differences such as these plague millions of children throughout America. Parents, teachers, and the students themselves often have little or no insight into the reasons why the children are failing, or how to manage their difficulties. So the children face daily public humiliation for the way they are wired, even though relatively easy and cost-effective means are available to help them.

The nonprofit institute *All Kinds of Minds* was founded in 1995 by Dr. Mel Levine to apply the latest neurodevelopmental research to the understanding and management of differences in learning. This is one of many institutes and organizations that provide families and teachers with a framework, a common language and tools, to enable this large, needy, and highly vulnerable segment of America's schoolchildren to become more successful learners.

Schools and districts are also continuing to work hard to provide the best assessment and learning techniques, as well as to train classroom teachers to help children with learning differences. Educators strive to ensure that children receive the individualized education that will help them enhance their innate strengths and overcome difficulties they may have encountered in school.

Recent scientific advances have provided us with a radically new understanding of variations in brain function. We must now apply that knowledge to help all kinds of minds contribute to our society in all kinds of constructive ways. We must acknowledge and celebrate this diversity of minds and learning challenges, and usher in a new era of learning.

Boys and Girls Learn Differently

Educator and author, Gurian and his co-writers (2002) argue that from preschool to high school, brain differences between the sexes call for different teaching strategies. The authors claim that until recently, society has taken the politically correct, but scientifically inaccurate, classroom view that children of both genders learn best in an "androgynous classroom." Presenting a detailed picture of boys' and girls' neurological, chemical, and hormonal disparities, the authors explain how those differences affect learning.

Although Gurian et al. address the problems of both genders, they focus on boys, contending that they are more difficult to teach and that they have more learning and discipline problems. The female brain, Gurian says, has a learning advantage because it is more complex and active, although the male brain does excel at abstract thinking and spatial relations, one reason why boys do better in math.

Chapter 13 discusses how education in schools today is changing, and how we must change with it. Establishing and maintaining a consistent environment that works provides lasting change as well as the ability to continue to meet the requirements needed to produce a quality academic program. In the twenty-first century, it is crucial that teachers be highly trained to meet the needs of our students today. This will result not only in a successful school, but also in the retention of your most qualified staff.

Chapter 14

Celebrating and Building Citizenship with Students

Paulo Freire (1970), Brazilian educator, stated, "A leader does not have to have all of the answers. Rather, a good leader has to make sure that all the right questions are on the table." Chapter 14 discusses how teaching is much more than just being in the classroom. Learning and teaching also involves looking holistically at the needs of our students and our community, such as in service-learning.

SERVICE-LEARNING

Service-learning is not a new term; in fact, it has been around for quite some time. But now seems like a good time to revisit this concept. Years ago, John F. Kennedy inspired a generation of youth to serve through civic initiatives such as the Peace Corps, inviting young people to rediscover their community and world awareness of peace, citizenship, and civic engagement.

Many educators are aware of this need still today. Doug Reeves (2006), education author and advisor to such national committees as the Council to Establish Academic Standards for Public Schools, stated in his book, *The Learning Leader*, that we need to find ways to restructure education so that we can create these much-needed systems of support and shared leadership within our schools, with programs such as service-learning.

The Chinese philosopher Lau Tse embodies the essence of the participatory approach to community service-learning development in this poem: "Go and meet your people, live and stay with them, love them, work with them. Begin with what they have, plan and develop from what they know, and in the end, when the work is over, they will say: 'we did it ourselves'" (Dennis 1977).

In his 2009 Inauguration Speech, President Barack Obama stated, "When you choose to serve, whether it's your nation, your community, or simply your neighborhood, you are connected to that fundamental American ideal that we want life, liberty and the pursuit of happiness not just for ourselves, but for all Americans. That's why it's called the American dream." Service-learning is a good program for the Me Generation. They are a group of people who are bright enough to be leaders for our future generations.

The term *service-learning* is defined as a teaching and learning strategy that integrates meaningful community service with instruction and reflection to enrich the learning experience, teach civic responsibility, and strengthen communities. The National Service-Learning Clearinghouse (1994) states, "An exciting, hands-on approach to education, service-learning, is taking place in a wide variety of settings: schools, universities, and community-based and faith-based organizations throughout the country."

Studies show students who participate in service-learning programs do better in school, are more likely to graduate high school and go to college, and are more likely to become active, engaged citizens. Schools that require or provide service-learning programs or opportunities as part of the educational experience create improved learning environments and serve as an important resource for their communities.

Community members, students, and educators everywhere are discovering that service-learning offers all its participants a chance to take part in the active education of its youth while simultaneously addressing the concerns, needs, and hopes of their community. Through service-learning, students are providing an important service to the community and at the same time are exposed to and learning about such community need areas such as water quality and laboratory analysis, developing an understanding of pollution issues, learning to interpret science issues to the public, and practicing communications skills by speaking to residents.

While involved, students reflect on their personal and career interests in science, the environment, public policy, or other related areas. In these ways, service-learning intentionally combines service with learning, a combination that is transforming both communities and students. The core concept driving this educational strategy is combining service objectives and learning objectives. Along with the intent to show measurable change in both the recipient and the provider of the service, the result is a radically effective transformative method of teaching students.

This is not to say that volunteer activities without a learning component are less important than service-learning—only that the two approaches are different activities with different objectives. Both are valued components of a national effort to increase citizen involvement in community service at every age.

In 2009, President Obama and Vice President Biden put out a charge to call on citizens of all ages to serve in some kind of service-learning. They set a goal for all middle school and high school students to engage in 50 hours of community service a year, and proposed a plan for all college students who engage in 100 hours of community service to receive a fully refundable tax credit of $4,000 for their education.

They also encouraged retiring Americans to serve by improving programs available for individuals over age 55, while at the same time promoting youth programs such as Youth Build and Head Start. With Baby Boomers predicted to retire in droves over the next decade, fears have been widespread in the public and nonprofit sectors that the United States will face a leadership shortage in many career fields, not just education.

President Obama (2009) recently stated in a speech, "I want to particularly say this to young people of every faith, in every country: you, more than anyone, have the ability to re-imagine the world, to remake this world." Being such an effective teaching and learning strategy, service-learning is often linked to school and college courses; however, it can also be organized and offered by community organizations as well.

Whatever the setting, according to the National Service-Learning Clearinghouse (1994), the core element of service-learning is always the intent that both providers and recipients find the experience beneficial, even transformative. There needs to be an underlying theme of emphasizing and showing empathy, sharing, caring, and consideration when performing service-learning.

Unfortunately, it seems a uniform society of showing empathy, sharing, caring, and consideration is dwindling. When was the last time that someone let you into traffic without flipping you off for cutting in front of them? Our society also needs to "get back to the basics" and learn to feel good about ourselves again by helping others and not just helping ourselves. There is something to be said about that feeling we get when we feel like we have helped someone. It feels good!

We should instill in our youth the value of service to the community and others at an early age. Starting out young and continuing this type of learning to help others will assist our society in becoming a caring, unified community again that is safe and healthy, and that produces the kind of community we all would want to live in.

Service-learning for the "Me" Generation

Service-learning is a great platform for the "Me" Generation to put some of their energies into transforming the public perception of marginalized youth by giving them a platform, a voice, and a cause. Teachers are just waiting for opportunities, and a rebirth in education to be able to put these young minds to work in "hands-on" learning—not only in the classrooms, but also in collaboration projects such as with their communities.

According to the National Service-Learning Clearinghouse (1994), a formalized service-learning program should include a rigorous student leadership development curriculum delivered by community leaders, practitioners, and educators, which would include the following concepts and characteristics of service-learning:

- Intensive weekly skill training and leadership development seminars
- Critical feedback, reflection, and personal coaching toward individual performance and professional goals
- Community building and team projects with a diverse cohort of peers
- Presentations of learning at the end of the year to demonstrate how one met the learning outcomes of the program

WHAT ARE THE CHARACTERISTICS OF SERVICE-LEARNING?

Authentic service-learning experiences, while almost endlessly diverse, have some common characteristics (taken mostly from Eyler & Giles, *Where's the Learning in Service-Learning?*, 1999):

- They are positive, meaningful, and real to the participants.
- They involve cooperative rather than competitive experiences and thus promote skills associated with teamwork and community involvement and citizenship.
- They address complex problems in complex settings rather than simplified problems in isolation.
- They offer opportunities to engage in problem-solving by requiring participants to gain knowledge of the specific context of their service-learning activity and community challenges, rather than only to draw upon generalized or abstract knowledge such as might come from a textbook. As a result, service-learning offers powerful opportunities to acquire the habits of critical thinking: that is, the ability to identify the most important questions or issues within a real-world situation.
- They promote deeper learning, because the results are immediate and uncontrived. There are no "right answers" in the back of the book.
- As a consequence of this immediacy of experience, service-learning is more likely to be personally meaningful to participants and to generate

emotional consequences, to challenge values as well as ideas, and hence to support social, emotional, and cognitive learning and development.

Examples of service-learning from the National Service-Learning Clearinghouse (2004) include the following:

- Elementary children in Florida studied the consequences of natural disasters. The class designed a kit for families to use to collect their important papers in case of evacuation with a checklist, tips about rescuing pets, and other advice to make a difficult situation easier, which students distributed to community members.
- Middle school students in Pennsylvania learned about the health consequences of poor nutrition and lack of exercise, and then brought their learning to life by conducting health fairs, creating a healthy cookbook, and opening a fresh fruit and vegetable stand for the school and community.
- Girl Scouts in West Virginia investigated the biological complexity and diversity of wetlands. Learning of the need to eliminate invasive species the scouts decided to monitor streams and ultimately presented their findings to their town council to raise awareness of issues concerning local wetlands.
- University students in Michigan looked for ways to support struggling local nonprofit organizations during difficult economic times. Graduate communication students honed their skills while providing a wide variety of public relations services with community partners, including developing press kits and managing event coordination.

President Obama stated in a March 26, 2009, speech, "[I]t is up to each of us to seize those opportunities, to do our part to lift up our fellow Americans, and to realize our own true potential. I call on all Americans to stand up and do what they can to serve their communities, shape our history and enrich both their own lives and the lives of others across this country." Leaders and educators everywhere are looking for some reprieve in education. It is more difficult now than ever before with the pressures of NCLB, the accountability movement, the high number of discipline problems, and the state of the economy. Educators are looking for ways to hang on and improve the situation at hand. Looking at the current situation in education and developing a plan to meet the overall needs will result in retaining your best educators and continuing to produce quality schools.

Chapter 15

Effective Teacher Evaluations: The New Performance-Based Model

At the beginning of the twenty-first century, not only do schools have more student testing than ever before, but education also has more teacher testing for various purposes than ever before. This chapter discusses a growing use of performance assessments of actual teaching for both formative purposes, such as during the induction period or a teacher's initial years of practice, and for summative purposes, such as for formal yearly evaluations for teachers or National Board Certification, all of which are continuing to be used, and promoted, to determine the effectiveness of teachers. The creation of the National Board for Professional Teaching Standards (NBPTS) in 1987 promoted discussion of more meaningful standards for teachers and resulted in developing a performance-based assessment system to recognize advanced competence among "experienced teachers."

This era was also the beginning of the development of a new teacher evaluation process based on teacher performance and is connected to student state test scores. This movement seems to be spreading nationwide. In some locations, it is a new evaluation process for instructional leaders as well.

The nation's first connected research this past year on the new evaluation model is from the state of Louisiana. The *ASCD* (Association for Supervisor and Curriculum Development) *SmartBrief* is posting articles online about this new model connecting teacher evaluations to teacher performance. The Obama administration is latching onto the concept and connecting it to the "Race to the Top" stimulus money. Many governors are signing bills that are changing how teachers are evaluated in states, starting as early as 2012. This movement results in teacher evaluations now being linked to a teacher's performance regarding students' state testing scores.

On May 28, 2010, the Louisiana State Department of Education adopted the Value-Added Teacher Evaluation Model through the passage of House Bill 1033. It was approved by the Louisiana Legislature and signed into law by Governor Bobby Jindal. This law links the evaluations of teachers and school administrators to student growth, and specifically calls for the annual evaluation of teachers and the statewide implementation of Louisiana's Value Added Assessment Model by the 2012–2013 school year.

The new Louisiana law calls for student academic growth to count for 50 percent of a teacher's evaluation. The remaining 50 percent is based on traditional methods. Louisiana's Value Added Formula is relying entirely on whether students meet predicted outcomes on state assessments to calculate the 50 percent student growth measure for teachers who teach tested grades and subjects, making it one of the most aggressive reform models in the nation. Socioeconomics, academic history, exceptionalities, and other factors will be used to predict how a student should learn in one year. In Louisiana, any teachers who are rated ineffective receive targeted professional development to help them improve. Any teacher rating "ineffective" three or more times during their certification cycle will not be recertified unless there is an appeal by the school board. Other measures of growth for nontesting teachers have not been stipulated yet.

A similar study was actually conducted from 1996 to 1998 about this subject. The "value-added" research, typified by the work of William Sanders and colleagues, reinforces the assumption that the teacher is the most significant factor that affects student achievement. Sanders' work in this area is the best known and is increasingly the most influential among policymakers. The study discussed how linking teacher performance and student achievement is both so intuitively compelling as a major part of a teacher's performance evaluation and so very difficult to implement that it has never really been systematically achieved in the United States. The pressure to forge such links is emerging, and governmental leaders see it as critical to the health and vitality of the educational system today.

In the decade from 1991 to 2001, a number of developments in public policy and assessment practices significantly altered the landscape for teacher evaluation practices. The single most important shift in the public policy arena is called "teacher accountability." What this seems to mean, in effect, is a growing insistence on measurement of teacher quality and teacher performance in terms of student achievement.

Those who are implementing these new programs think this is a huge step forward in making sure that every child is taught by an effective teacher, and that every public school is led by an effective instructional leader. Targeted professional development is identified as a major component of this new process. The belief is that this model enables school districts to identify and reward highly effective teachers and establish a mechanism for teachers and administrators to evaluate not only student progress but also teacher effectiveness. It allows teachers to see how they can improve on what works and change what does not. This new law does not necessarily affect teacher compensation; local districts remain in control over how teachers are rewarded and retained.

Other states, such as Oklahoma, recently approved similar models that not only incorporate student growth as a factor in teacher performance ratings, but also addresses incentive pay. Provisions are currently being developed for the introduction phase of the new method. Teacher unions around the country are not in support of this new legislation and idea. How is this new change going to affect our teachers, principals, and schools?

Many questions are still unanswered. The one question to address first is, What evaluation model or process will be used? Over the years, many states have looked at different kinds of evaluation processes and instruments to use for teacher evaluations. The new process being proposed needs to be very innovative and conclusive. Teacher evaluations currently are based on minimum criteria or state standards and are evaluation instruments consisting of a checklist and/or documents requiring brief written descriptions.

What will the new evaluation instrument look like? To really make this new process effective, the developers will want to undergo a process similar to a strategic plan: start with the end goal in mind. They should ask these following questions: What do we want teachers to do and accomplish? What kind of training should they have? What specific skills will be looked for? How will the new evaluation instrument address nontesting teachers?

In order to be effective, this process and instrument cannot be an evaluation of "an end product," but a teaching and reflective tool that is a collaborative effort between the teacher and the instructional leader. It has to serve as both a learning and growing tool to emphasize the lifelong learner and the process of continual growth as an educator. Effective teachers have to continue growing to be able to continue to be master teachers in the classroom each year, and in each new era that comes our way.

Undoubtedly, principals and teachers are frustrated with conventional evaluation practices, but are also scared about the new model being presented. The unknown is always scary when it is your job, and your life is in someone's hands. For evaluations, principals often use minimal teaching competencies associated with direct instruction as criteria to judge teachers' performance (Sclan 1994). This evaluation procedure runs the risk of becoming a meaningless exercise for the majority of teachers who are already performing at or beyond the minimal level (McLaughlin 1990; Searfoss & Enz 1996).

Traditional summative evaluation models are not necessarily structured to support dynamic, regenerative school environments. Evaluation procedures that focus on complying with regimented sets of behaviors do not encourage teacher involvement in their self-development or in the development of collaborative school cultures.

In order for the new teacher and leader evaluation to be comprehensive and a collaborative effort with the school district, it must address (1) what relationship there is between a teacher's practices and student learning, (2) what professional development interventions are likely to improve performance, (3) how the school and district support or detract from teachers' abilities to apply best professional practice, and (4) how the district supports or detracts from an evaluator's ability to conduct reliable and valid standards-based appraisals? Common ground should also be implemented to set up standards and definitions for what is considered effective teaching. For example,

- Teachers are committed to students and their learning
- Teachers know the subjects they teach and how to teach those subjects to students
- Teachers are responsible for managing and mentoring student learning
- Teachers think systematically about their practice and learn from experience
- Teachers are members of professional learning communities

Over the years, teacher preparation programs across the country have introduced evaluation instruments and processes that were standards-based and well-defined rubrics rather than discrete behaviors indicated by checklists. In these programs, the instructional leader plays a key role in modeling and communicating with the teacher. Portfolios and reflective processes are used to promote growth and self-reflection in the teacher. The research-based evaluation practices stress accountability and frequently reflects teacher-directed models of learning, such as lecture, demonstration, recitation, and modeling, designed primarily to transmit knowledge and cognitive skills to students.

Such evaluations often emphasize criteria derived from studies in the 1980s in which specific teaching behaviors in a direct instruction format predict high scores on standardized tests (Brophy & Good 1986). New systems that include evaluation as an authentic part of teachers' everyday practice with supports for regular reflection are naturally taking root as hierarchical controlling structures give way to environments that sustain collegial interactions (Sclan 1994).

During the last decade, an increasing number of teachers have been developing multidimensional, integrated learning environments where knowledge "depends on the values of the persons working with it and the context within which that work is conducted" (Lotto & Murphy 1990, p. 82, cited in Sclan 1994). Consistent with the goals of education for students to become lifelong learners and thoughtful decision makers in our democratic society, "constructivist" perspectives view schools as diverse learning communities where teachers must possess a broad repertoire of skills and knowledge consistent with the holistic needs of students (Dewey 1900 and 1902/1990). Direct instruction is only one of many useful teaching strategies, but it underlies traditional evaluation models, which are too narrow for assessing the performance of constructivist teachers or enhancing their practice.

Administrators and teachers need to access comprehensive evaluation models that capture the complexities of teaching today. Congruent with an expanding knowledge base of teaching and learning, performance standards are being developed that lead to reconfigured assessment designs requiring an array of reflective analytic skills.

The National Board for Professional Teaching Standards (NBPTS) recognizes that students learn by constructing new knowledge built on prior understandings and good teachers deliberate on the interaction of student strengths and needs, as well as learning contexts and content. NCTAF, which created a blueprint for recruiting, preparing, and supporting excellence in all of America's schools, recommends that the NBPTS's standards become the cornerstone for teacher evaluation (Darling-Hammond 1996; NCTAF 1996). The NBPTS's assessments help teachers reflect and learn from their practice.

The NBPTS and Interstate New Teacher Assessment and Support Consortium (INTASC) assessments are based on evidence of constructive practice and evaluate how specific teaching behaviors contribute to particular students' learning over time (NCTAF 1996). Using these guidelines, evaluation becomes part of a reflective process in which teaching is studied on a regular basis with colleagues for purposes of continual growth, rather than static formalities determined outside the classroom. A single observation or a principal's report alone provides an incomplete picture of what teachers do (Peterson 1990). Teaching needs to be understood dynamically in its multiple contexts, and performance data must be gathered from diverse sources.

As part of the movement toward more professionally grounded and performance-based standards for evaluation, several local and state initiatives incorporate peer review and assistance. These approaches appear to be more effective than traditional evaluation systems at both improving and letting go of teachers. The American Federation of Teachers (AFT) and the National Education Association (NEA) local affiliates have initiated peer review and assistance programs in districts across the United States. Because these systems rely on teachers' having increased opportunities for decision making and collaboration with colleagues, the process of evaluation becomes an integral part of everyday practice. Altering the process by which teachers are evaluated is providing the impetus for deeper structural changes in their responsibilities.

For example, through a rigorous process, a governing panel of teachers and administrators selects consulting teachers who mentor nontenured teachers and intervene with tenured teachers who are having difficulty. Along with increased autonomy comes greater accountability. In each program, standards have been strengthened for obtaining tenure and remaining in teaching (NCTAF 1996). According to NCTAF (1996), the success of peer review and assistance programs can be attributed to (1) more useful measures of performance, (2) intensive assistance, and (3) expertise of the consulting teachers, who are matched by subject area and grade level with the teacher being helped.

Although evaluating and rewarding teacher performance is arguably a local school or district responsibility, the matter of removing incompetent teachers has received attention from the federal government. During 1997 and 1998, as Congress considered amendments to the Higher Education Act, lawmakers noted the need for administrators to remove unqualified teachers and included provisions to allow states to use federal funds to offer teachers professional development opportunities and to "expeditiously remove incompetent or unqualified teachers" (Higher Education Amendments of 1998, Title II. Sec. 202(d)(5)).

This historical information about educator evaluation processes will provide the next generation of evaluation systems further information to consider and integrate into methods of teacher accountability with professional growth. Eisner (1992) conceives of evaluation as inherently part of teachers' everyday work life. Evaluation needs to be participatory and reflective in order to be meaningful for teachers. Reform of teacher evaluation systems is already supporting the success of broader school reform efforts, which include the requirements of teachers' evolving roles. The goal of these changes is meaningful learning experiences for our children.

A set of model performance-based licensing standards for "new teachers" compatible with the NBPTS's certification standards has been developed by INTASC, a program of the Council of Chief State School Officers. Working in collaboration with teachers and teacher educators, state licensing officials, National Council for the Accreditation of Teacher Education (NCATE), and other stakeholders, INTASC has created a set of core standards that define the knowledge, dispositions, and performances essential for all beginning teachers (INTASC 1992).

Thirty-three states are participating in translating the ten core standards into discipline-specific standards in each of the major K–12 content areas. Eleven of these states are piloting prototype performance assessments (INTASC 1995, 1996). The new assessments are modeled on NBPTS's portfolios, which include videotapes and analysis of teaching, samples of lessons, assignments, and student work. Teachers are asked to demonstrate how their teaching relates to their students' learning. The assessments are also matched with new standards for each discipline (e.g., the new National Council for Teachers of Mathematics standards). In the pilot assessments, teachers provide evidence of how they foster higher-level reasoning and problem-solving skills (NCTAF 1996).

Chapter 15 reiterates how the new twenty-first-century teacher performance evaluation system must include a high-quality mentoring and focused professional development program that will increase the skills of the evaluee. Elements of the program should include enhancing the capacity of mentors to coach the teachers in need, a system in place that would retain beginning teachers and improving their instructional quality, creating high-functioning professional learning communities, developing teachers into high-quality professionals who improve student learning, and developing principals into high-performing instructional leaders. Not only should this new system include expected behaviors and skills, but it should also contain a mechanism of self-reflection and application. Such a process will assist in retaining the most effective teachers and principals in our schools today by developing professionally qualified educators who are prepared to teach and lead.

Conclusion

A teacher friend of mine came to me recently wanting help and new solutions to the new problems with our current generation, affectionately called the "Me" Generation. Teachers and principals all over the nation are struggling with lots of discipline and violence issues, behavior problems, high-stress testing with No Child Left Behind, and the economical situation and its effects on education today.

How to Keep Good Teachers and Principals offers a unique understanding of what is going on in education in the classrooms as well as in the overall schools. This book will provide life-saving strategies and answers to the questions educators have these days about what is going on, and what they can do about it. New ways of solving the problems with classroom management and behavior are posed in the chapters through model and practice techniques, while also sparking ideas for organizing the classroom, using authentic learning and technology to inspire students, implementing service-learning to provide students with leadership skills that will help them to be responsible citizens of their school and community, and other practical and hands-on methods that are doable for any educator or leader. This book will hopefully provide educators in the twenty-first century with methods of dealing with the new challenges that face teachers and principals.

Appendix A

Table A.1. Stress Scale

Stressor	Stress level	Stressor	Stress level	Stressor	Stress level
Parent dies	100	New extracurricular activity	36	Trouble with teacher	24
Parents divorce	73			Change in child-care hours	20
Parents separate	65	Change in number of fights with siblings	35	Changes to a new school	20
Parent travels as part of job	63	Fears violence at school	31	Changes play habits	19
Close family member dies	63	Theft of personal possessions	30	Vacations with family	19
Personal illness or injury	53	Changes in responsibilities at home	29	Changes friends	18
Parent remarries	50			Attends summer camp	17
Parent fired from job	47	Older sibling leaves home	29	Changes sleeping habits	16
Parents reconcile	45	Trouble with grandparents	29	More or fewer family gatherings	15
Mother goes to work	45				
Mother becomes pregnant	40	Outstanding achievement	28	Changes eating habits	15
School difficulties	39	Move to another city	26	Changes in the amount of television viewing	13
Birth of a sibling	39	Move to another part of town	26	Birthday party	12
New teacher or class	39			Punished for lying	11
Change in family finances	38	Receives or loses a pet	25		
Close friend is hurt or ill	37	Changes personal habits	24		

Source: Elkind (1986).
Note: This scale estimates the impact of various changes in children's lives. Add up the points for all the changes your child has experienced in the last year. Scores below 150 are about average. Children with scores between 150 and 300 have a better-than-average chance of showing some symptoms of stress. If your child's score is above 300, there is a strong likelihood that he or she will experience a serious health or behavior problem.

Bibliography

Barth, Roland. *Improving Schools from Within: Teachers, Parents, and Principals Can Make a Difference.* San Francisco: Jossey-Bass, 1990.

Breaux, Annette. "Induction Programs Help Keep Better Teachers," *Education World* (August 21, 2003), www.educationworld.com/a_issues/chat/chat071.shtml.

Brophy, Jere, and Tom Good. "Teacher Behavior and Student Achievement." In Merlin Wittrock (ed.), *Handbook of Research on Teaching,* New York: MacMillan, 1986.

Business Roundtable. *Effective Leadership on the World Stage,* 2009, www.businessroundtable.org.

Center for Public Education. "Measuring Student Growth: At a Glance." Alexandria, Virginia (2007), www.centerforpubliceeducation.org/site/app/nlnet/Content3.aspx?c=lvIXIiN0JwE&b=5119575&content_id=(9BA6BD92-A81A-4891-B77E-77029506B39D)&notoc=1.

Cognition and Technology Group at Vanderbilt. "Designing Learning Environments That Support Thinking: The Jasper Series as a Case Study." In Thomas Duffy, Joost Lowyck, and David Jonassen (eds.), *Designing Environments for Constructive Learning.* New York: Springer-Verlag, 1993.

Darling-Hammond, Linda. *Doing What Matters Most: Investing in Quality Teaching.* New York: National Commission on Teaching & America's Future, 1997.

Devaney, Laura. "Let Retiring Boomers Transform Schools," *School News* (2009), www.eschoolnews.com/2009/07/22/let-retiring-boomers-transform-schools/.

Dewey, John. *The School and Society and the Child and the Curriculum.* Chicago: University of Chicago Press, 1990.

Dickson, Dee. "Questions to Neuroscientists from Educators," *New Horizons* (2000), http://newhorizons.org/neuro/dickinson_questions.htm.

DuFour, Richard. "Schools as Learning Communities." *Educational Leadership,* *61*(8) (2004): 6–11.

DuFour, Richard, and Robert Eaker. *Professional Learning Communities at Work: Best Practices for Enhancing Student Achievement*. Bloomington, IN: National Educational Service, 1998.

Eastern Mennonite University. *What Is the Conceptual Framework of the Teacher? Education Unit* (1996), www.emu.edu/education/model.htmle (site now discontinued).

Eisner, Elliot. "Educational Reform and the Ecology of Schooling." *Teachers College Record* (1992): 610–627.

Engineer, Nazer, Cherie Percaccio, and Michael Kilgard. "Environment Shape Auditory Processing," *New Horizons* (2004), www.newhorizons.org/neuro/engineer%20percaccio%20kilgard.htm.

Evans, Kelly. "Real Time Economics," 2009, http://blogs.wsj.com/economics/2009/11/10/as-unemployment-rises-kids-future-dims/.

Eyler, Janet, and Dwight Giles. "What Are the Characteristics of Service-Learning?" 1999, www.servicelearning.org/what_is_service-learning/characteristics/index.php.

Faye, Jim. "Love and Logic," 2009, www.loveandlogic.com.

Freire, Paulo. "Pedagogy of the Oppressed," 1970, www.education.miami.edu/ep/contemporaryed/Paulo_Freire/paulo_freire.html.

Fullan, Michael. *Change Forces: The Sequel*. New York: Falmer Press, 1999.

Gupton, Sandra. *The Instructional Leadership Toolbox*. Thousand Oaks, CA: Corwin Press, Inc., 2003.

Gurian, Michael. *Boys and Girls Learn Differently!: A Guide for Teachers and Parents*. San Francisco: Jossey Bass, 2002.

Harris, Kevin. "Collected Quotes From Albert Einstein," 1995, http://rescomp.stanford.edu/~cheshire/EinsteinQuotes.html.

Heflin, Juan, and Paul Alberto. "Establishing a Behavioral Context for Learning for Students with Autism." *Focus on Autism and Other Developmental Disabilities*, 16(2) (July 2005): 93–102.

Holmes, Thomas, and Richard Rahe. "Homes-Rahe Social Readjustment Rating Scale." *Journal of Psychosomatic Research*, *11*(2) (1967): 213–218.

Hume, Kara. "Clean Up Your Act! Creating an Organized Classroom Environment for Students on the Spectrum." *The Reporter, 13*(1) (2007): 15–18.

Hurth, Joicey, Evelyn Shaw, Susan Izeman, Kathy Whaley, and Sally Rogers. "Areas of Agreement about Effective Practices among Programs Serving Young Children with Autism Spectrum Disorders." *Infants and Young Children, 12*(2) (October 1999): 17–26.

Interstate New Teacher Assessment and Support Consortium. *Model Standards for Beginning Teacher Licensing and Development*. Washington, DC: Council of Chief State School Officers, 1992.

Interstate New Teacher Assessment and Support Consortium, Mathematics Sub-Committee. *Model Standards in Mathematics for Beginning Teacher Licensing and Development*. Washington, DC: Council of Chief State School Officers, 1995.

Interstate New Teacher Assessment and Support Consortium. *The INTASC Performance Assessment Development Project*. Washington, DC: Council of Chief State School Officers, 1996.

Interstate New Teacher Assessment and Support Consortium. *Next Steps: Moving toward Performance-Based Licensing in Teaching.* Washington, DC: Council of Chief State School Officers, 1990.
Keefe, James, and John Jenkins. "Two Schools: Two Approaches to Personalized Learning." *Phi Delta Kappan, 83*(6) (February 2002): 449–456.
Lebow, David. "Authentic Activity as a Model for Appropriate Learning Activity: Implications for Emerging Instructional Technologies." *Canadian Journal of Educational Communication, 23*(3) (1994): 231–244.
Levine, Mel. "Misunderstood Minds," *New Horizons* (2002), www.newhorizons.org/neuro/levine.htm.
Lewis, Beth. "Class Meetings Help Foster Responsible, Ethical Student Behavior," 2009, http://k6educators.about.com/od/classroommanagement/a/communitycircs.htm.
Lieberman, Ann. "Practices That Support Teacher Development." *Phi Delta Kappan, 76* (April 1995): 591–596.
McLaughlin, Mary. "Embracing Contraries: Implementing and Sustaining Teacher Evaluation." In Jason Millman and Linda Darling-Hammond (eds.), *The New Handbook of Teacher Evaluation.* Newbury Park, CA: Sage, 1990.
Mesibov, Gary, Victor Shea, and Eric Schopler. *The TEACCH Approach to Autism Spectrum Disorders.* New York: Kluwer Academic, 2005.
Michigan Department of Education. *What Research Says about Parent Involvement in Children's Education in Relation to Academic Achievement,* 2002, www.michigan.gov/documents/Final_Parent_Involvement_Fact_Sheet_14732_7.pdf.
Moore, Robin C., and Herbert Wong. *Natural Learning: The Life History of an Environmental Schoolyard.* Berkeley, CA: MIG Communications, 1997.
National Board for Professional Teaching Standards. *Toward High and Rigorous Standards for the Teaching Profession.* Detroit: National Board for Professional Teaching Standards, 1989.
National Board for Professional Teaching Standards. *An Invitation to National Board Certification.* Southfield, MI: National Board for Professional Teaching Standards, 1997.
National Commission on Teaching and America's Future. *What Matters Most: Teaching for America's Future.* Washington, DC: National Commission on Teaching and America's Future, 1996.
National Commission on Teaching and America's Future. *Learning Teams Creating What Is Next.* Washington, DC: National Commission on Teaching and America's Future, 2009.
National Service-Learning Clearinghouse. *Defining Service-Learning,* 1995, www.servicelearning.org/what_is_service-learning/service-learning_is/index.php.
National Service Learning Clearinghouse. *What Is Service-Learning?,* 2009, www.servicelearning.org/what_is_service-learning/service-learning_is/index.php.
National Youth Network. *Behavior Modification–Child Behavior Problems–Out of Control Teens–Behavior Modification Schools,* 2009, www.nationalyouth.com/behaviormodification.html.

Obama, Barack. *The Inauguration Speech*, January 20, 2009, http://change.gov/americaserves/.
Ohanian, Susan. *Commentaries*, 2003, www.susanohanian.org/?page=194.
Ohanian, Susan. *What Happened to Recess and Why Are Our Children Struggling in Kindergarten?* New York: McGraw Hill, 2002.
Ornstein, Allan. "How to Recognize Good Teaching." *The American School Board Journal*, *180*(1) (1993): 24–27.
Pellegrini, Anthony. *Recess: Its Role in Education and Development*. Mahwah, NJ: Erlbaum, 2005.
Pellegrini, Anthony, and Paul Davis. "Relations between Children's Playground and Classroom Behavior." *British Journal Of Educational Psychology*, *63*(1) (1993): 88–95.
Pope, Tara. "The 3 R's? A Fourth Is Crucial, Too: Recess," *New York Times* (February 23, 2009), www.nytimes.com/2009/02/24/health/24well.html?_r=1.
Potthast, Amy. *President Obama on the Serve America Act*, 2009, http://thenewservice.wordpress.com/tag/president-obama/.
Potthast, Amy. *President Obama and Government Careers*, 2009, http://thenewservice.wordpress.com/tag/president-obama/.
Potthast, Amy. *Senate Approves Funding for Peace Corps and AmeriCorp Programs*, 2009, http://thenewservice.wordpress.com/tag/president-obama/.
Presidential Task Force on Psychology in Education, and American Psychological Association. *Learner-Centered Psychological Principles: Guidelines for School Design and Reform*. Washington, DC: American Psychological Association/Mid-continent Regional Educational Laboratory, 1993.
Pytel, Barbara. "Recess Becoming Obsolete—Schools Are Cutting Recess Time," 2006, http://educationalissues.suite101.com/article.cfm/recess_becoming_obsolete.
Rockman et al. *Authentic Learning and Technology*, 1995, www.rockman.com/articles/AuthenticLearning.htm.
Schwahn, Chuck. *Total Leaders: Applying the Best Future-Focused Change Strategies to Education*. Arlington, VA: American Association of School Administrators, 1998.
Sclan, Eileen. *Performance Evaluation for Experienced Teachers: An Overview of State Policies*. Washington, DC: ERIC Clearinghouse on Teaching and Teacher Education, 1994.
Searfoss, Lyndon, and Billie Enz. "Can Teacher Evaluation Reflect Holistic Instruction?" *Educational Leadership*, *53*(6) (March 1996): 38–41.
Senge, Peter. *The Fifth Discipline: The Art and Practice of the Learning Organization*. New York: Currency Doubleday, 1990.
Sergiovanni, Thomas. *The Principalship: A Reflective Practice Perspective* (2nd ed.). Needham Heights, MA: Ally & Bacon, 1991.
Sergiovanni, Thomas, and Robert Starratt. *Supervision: Human Perspectives* (3rd ed.). New York: McGraw-Hill, 1988.
Sergiovanni, Thomas. "Ten Principles of Quality Leadership." *Educational Leadership*, *39*(5) (2002): 330–335.

Shapiro, Edward, and Christine Cole. *Behavior Change in the Classroom: Self-Management Interventions*. New York, NY: Guilford Press, 1994.
Styles, Donna. "A Democratic Approach to Classroom Management." *Education World* (2009), www.educationworld.com/a_curr/profdev/profdev012.shtml.
TeacherVision. "Class Meeting," 2009, www.teachervision.fen.com/classroom-management/interpersonal-skills/4864.html?page=2&detoured=1.
Tomlinson, Carol. *How to Differentiate Instruction in Mixed Ability Classrooms*. Alexandria, VA: Association for Supervision and Curriculum Development, 2004.
Tulsa Public Schools. *Tulsa Area Community Schools Initiative*, 2010, www.csctulsa.org/community_schools.htm.
Wong, Harry, and Rosemary Wong. *The First Days of School: How to Be an Effective Teacher*. Mountain View, CA: Harry K. Wong Publications, Inc., 2001.

About the Author

Dr. Lonnie Melvin shares a powerful vision for teaching and learning and has a wealth of knowledge to share with anyone working in education today. Her varied experiences as an educational leader, counselor, teacher, and college professor, as well as experience with inpatient and outpatient mental health centers and with special education, allows her to present this much-needed information about new educational practices in logical and practical ways. Dr. Melvin was named an Oklahoma Association of Elementary School Principals (OAESP) District 7D District Administrator of the Year in 2008 and two of her schools were named as a Model Best Practice School in Oklahoma in 2004. Her 26 years of experience in education allow her to have the background needed to write this book and introduce her own coined version of a new behavior modification model called Self-Correcting Behavior Modification.

www.ingramcontent.com/pod-product-compliance
Lightning Source LLC
Chambersburg PA
CBHW032030230426
43671CB00005B/267